Putting
heads
on beds

More related titles

Just Six Guests
*First-hand, encouraging advice on how to set up
and run a small Bed and Breakfast*

Starting & Running a B&B
'Would-be and current B&B owners are given a short
course on everything they need to know to make their
property a special place to stay – from buying an
established B&B to day-to-day operations.' – *Active Life*

Buying & Running a Small Hotel
'Brimming with essential information ... required reading for
those newly entering the business.' – Tourism Business
Adviser, Business Link

The Small Business Start-up Workbook
A step-by-step book to starting the business you've dreamed of

'I would urge every business adviser in the land to
read this incredibly useful, well-written and informative
book ... Full of invaluable advice!' – *The Daily Telegraph*

howtobooks

Send for a free copy of the latest catalogue to:

How To Books
3 Newtec Place, Magdalen Road,
Oxford OX4 1RE, United Kingdom
email: info@howtobooks.co.uk
http://www.howtobooks.co.uk

Putting
heads
on beds

The complete practical
guide to marketing your
independent hotel or
guest accommodation

Michael Cockman

howto**books**

Published by How To Books Ltd
3 Newtec Place, Magdalen Road
Oxford OX4 1RE, United Kingdom
Tel: (01865) 793806. Fax: (01865) 248780
email: info@howtobooks.co.uk
www.howtobooks.co.uk

British Library Cataloguing in Publication Data
A catalogue record for this book is available from the British Library

Cover design by Baseline Arts Ltd, Oxford
Produced for How To Books by Deer Park Productions, Tavistock
Typeset by PDQ Typesetting, Newcastle-under-Lyme, Staffs.
Printed and bound by Cromwell Press, Trowbridge, Wiltshire

NOTE: The material contained in this book is set out in good faith for general
guidance and no liability can be accepted for loss or expense incurred as a result
of relying in particular circumstances on statements made in the book. The laws
and regulations are complex and liable to change, and readers should check the
current position with the relevant authorities before making personal
arrangements.

Contents

Dedication   vii

Acknowledgements   ix

Preface   xi

Introduction   xiii

Part 1 – Getting Started   1

1   Where Are You Now?   3
    What does your hotel look like?   3
    Does your product suit the market?   15
    How does the competition compare?   30

2   Where Do You Want To Be?   37
    What is your vision for the future?   37
    What types of customer are available?   44
    What channels can you use to reach them?   63

3   What Help Do You Need?   76
    What is your leadership style?   76
    Should you employ a sales specialist?   87
    How can you create a committed team?   93
    What incentives can you use?   114

Part 2 – Reaching Your Prospects   119

4   Using Personal Contact   121
    Telephone   121
    Direct contact   129
    Networking   147

5   Direct Marketing   150
    Direct mail   150
    E-mail   160
    Newsletters   165

6   Advertising   170
    Is advertising relevant for me?   170

7   **Media Relations**   183
    Worth the effort   183

8   **Promotional Materials and Activity**   194
    Sales promotion   194
    Brochures   201
    Your internet site   206

Part 3 – Getting Where You Want To Be   229

9   **How Do You Price To Maximise Revenue?**   231
    Pricing challenges   231
    Yield management   243

10 **How Do You Make Systems and Data Work For
    You?**   250
    How to measure customer satisfaction   250
    Useful data to keep   257
    Implement systems for an easier life   268

11 **What Tactics Can You Use To Develop Revenue?**   281
    Customer evaluation   281
    Increasing revenue   284

12 **Planning Your Marketing Activity**   290
    What is left to do?   290
    Marketing plan format   293
    The last word   303

Resources   307

Further reading   309

Index   311

Dedication

This book is dedicated to the memory of John Mackinlay (1939–2005) latterly Managing Director of Hotel Management International (HMI) Ltd. He was an inspiration not only to me but also to all the many people who came into contact with him. He will be missed by us all but particularly by his family.

Acknowledgements

A childhood fascination with aeroplanes took me to British Airways, where I probably worked for more years than I should have. But I learnt a great deal that I was able to put to good use later on. It was Jacques Schneider of Profile who eventually persuaded me to try for a job in the hotel industry where Michael Holland was my initial great influence at The Gloucester Hotel (now the Millennium Gloucester). Tim Stableforth came all the way from New Zealand to persuade me (admittedly without much difficulty) to take a marketing role that included covering Fiji and Tahiti. When I returned to the UK, John Mackinlay of HMI took the same approach except that the hotel in the Caribbean was disposed of soon after I started!

In putting together this practical guide for owners and managers of independent hotels and guest accommodation I would like to acknowledge the assistance of the team at theHotelCoach; everyone at How to Books, particularly Melanie Jarman who has been a very kind and helpful editor; all the people I have coached and mentored over the years and those that I have interviewed during my research. With special thanks to Carol Whitaker, Martin Philips, Steve Alexander, Jacque Richardson and Peter Cockman for invaluable help with checking technical aspects of the text.

Preface

A book like this has some unique challenges for the reader. Unlike a John Le Carré novel there is not much of a story to pull you from one page to the next; the tension does not really build in the same way. However, you have bought the book and presumably you really do intend to read it and not put it on your bookshelf along with *A Brief History of Time* as a project for another day.

Like any novel, this book does have a sort of logic to it. I will ask you to look at where you are now, decide where you want to get to, and I will give you some ideas about how you might get there. The implication of this process is that some change is required; indeed only by changing what you do now will you have any chance of achieving outcomes that are different to those that you now experience.

I wrote this book as a practical guide for owners and managers of any independent accommodation business. It sets down some of the sales and marketing tools and techniques that are available to help you develop your business. It doesn't matter whether you have a large or small hotel or call yourself a hotel, pub, bed and breakfast or guesthouse; you might also be a college or training centre. The challenges are all the same.

I hope that this book will also be useful to sales executives that are new to hospitality and need to understand how the business works.

Don't worry; this is not a theoretical book about 'marketing'. There will be no marketing definitions and certainly no esoteric discussions about whether you need to look at the five or seven 'P's of marketing. I have not included any graphs or charts and I hope that you won't find this a drawback. I have also deliberately not included sample advertisements, direct mail letters, brochures or internet sites. My reasoning here is that I want you to learn techniques that will enable you to produce great material for yourself; there are far too many 'me too' approaches in the hotel business and much of what is copied was not very good in the first place! This book is however definitely *about* marketing, explaining some of the tactics that can help fill your hotel rooms and generate extra revenue.

Although much hospitality training and education is still regrettably very product focused, the influence of sales and marketing within the hospitality business has changed for the better over the years. When I first started in the hotel business 25 years ago I joined a hotel, with over 500 rooms, that in the 10 years since it opened had not had a full-time sales manager: the activity had been covered by trainees on rotation! Contrast this with my last company where over 50 per cent of general managers were ex-sales managers.

I understand why you may not be in a position to make sales development your first priority but, hopefully, by the end of our time together I will have persuaded you that the subject is too important to put on the back burner.

Although I was very daunted by the thought of writing this book, I am a little sad to have completed it. I hope that you enjoy reading it as much as I enjoyed writing it.

Michael Cockman

Introduction

If you provide hospitality to travellers you are continuing a very ancient calling. Nowadays you don't have to send your over-booking to a stable, but the essentials of the business remain the same. What has changed and continues to influence your business are the new and different aspirations of both your customers and your guests.

The activities of some of the listed hotel groups and investment vehicles make for very interesting reading, as does the changing role of the internet as a distribution medium. However we get so caught up in providing the latest amenity to score over our competitor that we sometimes forget that what we should really be focusing on is satisfying customers and guests by solving their problems.

In my opinion there are some major influences that form the background against which you manage your hospitality business.

BRANDS

The meaning of the word 'brand' or 'branding' can change with the context, and sometimes brand is a verb and sometimes a noun. For some people it is a trademark (brand name) and for others it is the embodiment of their expectations from a service or company. Whatever it is, a brand becomes something that people trust, and branding is about making an emotional connection with your customer or guest. A company or organisation can develop a successful brand but the value of the brand is all in the mind of the customer.

Although brands have been around since the advent of packaged goods in the 19th century, it is not long ago that brands became associated with every type of service too. At no time has there been such a fixation on brands as a means of defining oneself. We now accept that the label is on the outside of our clothes. The new generation of purchasers select their experiences and consumer goods on a different basis to that of their predecessors.

There are many easily recognisable brands such as Apple, Coca-Cola, Calvin Klein, BMW, Nokia and Nintendo, all with worldwide sales. Maybe you are wondering what this has got to do with your hotel? As I said before, the new generation of customers is much more aware of brands and will appreciate your efforts to be consistent with your promise as embodied in your brand. Your brand is the way that you differentiate yourself and show that you have made the effort to align your service with the expectations of your customer. You can learn from some of these global companies in the consistent way that they portray their organisations and in the way that 'personality' can be attached to products and services. Another bonus of working on your own brand is that branded services also generally command higher prices.

STAFFING

Whenever I talk to owners or managers about increasing sales it is not long before the conversation comes around to the difficulties of delivering customer service because of the general lack of commitment from staff.

Is this a general lack of motivation by employees or do we just not understand that their work ethic may be different to previous generations? The young people we are talking about are probably those born between 1976 and 1994 and are variously referred to as 'Generation Y', 'Thatcher's Children' or the 'Echo Generation'; maybe Don Tapscott's (*Growing Up Digital*) term the 'Net

Generation' is more appropriate since they have grown up immersed in a digital and internet-driven world. They have also seen that dedication and obedience to your employer does not always bring rewards: their parents are likely to have had more than one job and may well have been made redundant, maybe more than once. What price loyalty?

They also know that, in the new culture of celebrity, hard work is not necessarily the quickest route to financial rewards. If you are in the right place at the right time you can take a shortcut, even if it is via *Big Brother*!

The education system has changed, with much less need to keep information in your head. The most important attribute now is knowing where to look for that information. But this generation does seem to be better at multi-tasking: possibly the product of a lack of concentration? They can think fast and are often creative. It is against this background that you have to construct your own methods of working with your staff. They do not need to be managed much differently from any other group before them. Just let them know that what they do matters, explain everything in detail, be open with your communication, give them responsibility, praise them, set a good example and make their work day fun. Easy really!

CUSTOMERS

Although it is not possible to pinpoint exactly, it seems likely that an increasing number of your guests will be those born in the period 1964–1976 and referred to as 'Generation X'. Due to the falling birth rate, there are fewer of them than their parents, the Baby Boomers (1946–1964) from the post-war period, but there is now a greater proportion of women in the workforce, continuing the post-war trend. They have embraced new technology but they also remember the time before the PC and the DVD player.

This generation have embraced brands wholeheartedly, maybe in rebellion at their parent's sensible choices based on utility and longevity. They embrace risk and prefer to be freelance rather than stuck in a corporate hierarchy: they were the architects of the dot.com boom.

The development of the boutique hotel has coincided with their rise through business organisations. This product customisation has appealed to their quest for emotional security, independence and informality. Yet now that the large international groups are rolling out 'boutique' hotels, has this particular segment had its day?

The attitudes of this customer group will impact on your business in some way. What you do about it depends on your willingness to listen to what they want and how far you want to go to provide it. Is it economically viable?

THE INTERNET

The development of the internet has had a huge impact on the hotel business and will continue to influence the way that you do business. There are now many new ways to distribute your rooms, increasing the transparency of whatever you do. There is also a disturbing reliance on room rate as a measure of quality.

There was a time when the key to successful hotel keeping was preventing your various market segments finding out the rates that each was given. I remember when I first started in the business we used to get very upset when a tour operator started to book corporate guests at the group rate we had given him. Now that I think about it, it wasn't really his fault: we just omitted to put in the right conditions that erected the right 'fence'.

The conventional complicated rate structure is now very difficult to sustain. You have to think through any action very carefully so that you keep control of the rate initiative. Corporate clients are very willing to cancel their reservations and rebook at the special internet rates if these undercut their rate.

Third-party suppliers have become very powerful but their sites make it extremely difficult to get across the quality of your product, so that rate becomes the only judge of quality. This will have to change if they are to continue to play a valuable role in your distribution mix.

As you generate more and more business through the internet you will need to make some key management decisions. All these new distribution channels plus the needs of your own website demand a high degree of technical expertise and a major daily time commitment. Can you afford to develop in-house expertise or is this an area where outsourcing makes sense?

MARKETING AND HOTELS

Those of you who have worked in the chain or franchise sector will have become a little perplexed by the different ways that each company organises itself to generate sales revenue. The process is often broken down into sales, marketing and revenue management and much corporate energy is spent on internal disputes and arguments about who is responsible for what and to whom. Even the sales organisation is disrupted every so often, responding to the latest trend in clusters, regions or individual accountability.

As an independent operator you have the choice to make a sensible organisation that is simply focused on the task in hand. You have no need for arbitrary organisation divisions and can allocate tasks to the most appropriate person in your team. You can take a much more creative approach to investing money both in developing new business and keeping the business you have, knowing that you have in place the right systems to measure the benefits from any particular action.

The other benefit of the independent operator is that you are not so bound by the short-termism of the City, with its expectations that the profit in each 12 months will definitely be better than the last, whatever the cost. You know that growth strategies sometimes take a long time to reach fruition.

Marketing activities need the same disciplines applied as any other of the other business activities:

♦ **Leadership:** This can be from the front or from behind, however you decide to set up your organisation (explored in Chapter 3) but however you do it you need to be decisive and inclusive. Effective leadership gives forward momentum to the business, without which it will ultimately fail. Imagine an aeroplane without such forward momentum; it would definitely fall out of the sky.

♦ **Buy-in:** Nothing will work unless you gain complete commitment from your team members (see Chapter 3) since they have to deliver what you promise and at the same time be a part of the wider sales team.

- **Consistency**: Building a successful rooms business is a long-term exercise. Whether it is building relationships or advertising, no action is effective unless you give it enough time to work (explored in Part 2). Of course you need to measure what you do but sticking to your plan is vital.

- **Relevancy**: Although this may appear to be an obvious concept, it is now more vital than ever that you analyse every activity for its relevancy to your target market. Customers are assaulted by so many messages that if you don't accurately target messages that are relevant you will lose your opportunity to communicate. It is also imperative that any new initiatives are relevant to delivering exceptional customer service; it is no good investing in new facilities or campaigns if you haven't empowered your team and secured their buy-in.

What marketing should do above all is enhance 'shareholder value'. It does this by you investing appropriate funds in tactics that lead to increases in operating profit and thus your asset value. This profit (earnings before interest, tax and depreciation) is directly affected by your ability to:

- retain the customers you have;
- increase their average rate/spend;
- persuade them to buy more often;
- attract new customers.

Everything in this book will involve one or more of these growth opportunities.

Part One
Getting Started

Chapter 1 Where Are You Now?
What does your hotel look like?
Does your product suit the market?
How does the competition compare?

Chapter 2 Where Do You Want To Be?
What is your vision for the future?
What types of customer are available?
What channels can you use to reach them?

Chapter 3 What Help Do You Need?
What is your leadership style?
Should you employ a sales specialist?
How can you create a committed team?
What incentive can you use?

'Understand you're not God. You cannot do everything yourself and you have to trust other people.'

Raymond Blanc

1

Where Are You Now?

Knowing where you are and where you are going are two vital aspects of the planning cycle. Never feel that you have a product and that you are stuck with it, whatever the competition does.

WHAT DOES YOUR HOTEL LOOK LIKE?

I am amazed every day as I travel around just how little attention is paid by some hospitality operators to how their business is portrayed: do these people walk around with their eyes closed?

This is particularly surprising when you consider how much emphasis is put on image. I use image in its widest sense, not to imply glamour or fashion but image as in reflecting what your business is about. Often it's the small things that count – the badly written A-board, the long forgotten broken sign in a field or just the weeds in the front garden. Talking of A-boards, why is it that white chalk on a blackboard indicates something more up-market than a mixture of blue, red and green chalk on the same board? There are many tools and techniques available to give your customers a positive impression of your operation.

The influences of design, maintenance, colour, fonts, typography and text are many and various and I will try to clarify some of the most important issues. Although it is easy to dismiss the activities of Nike, Red Bull, Apple, Ford or Virgin as being of no relevance to your operation, there are some fundamentals that apply whatever your business.

Time to make an impression

How long do you have to make a first impression? Some research indicates that it is no more than 20 seconds. In that time your prospect has had a chance to view your product and weigh up in his or her mind whether or not it meets their expectations.

Corporate identity

You might be thinking that a section on corporate identity has little application to an individual hotel. Large companies spend a huge amount of money on identity and although it is sometimes more about a 'new look' to paper over cracks in their operation, there is a lot to be learnt about how others do it. You don't have to follow everything to the letter, but some of the techniques have a universal application.

◆ TIP ◆

A corporate identity programme encompasses all that your potential customers will see about your hotel and involves your choice of name, colour, logo, typeface, paper and copy style.

Once you have set out your vision (see page 37), your corporate identity is what translates it into reality. But before you can do this you need to reflect on how you wish to position yourself. You need to determine your position in your customers' minds, taking into account the needs of your customers, the strengths and weaknesses of your hotel and your position in relation to your competition. You need to agree on the market segments that you wish to serve so that your corporate identity is congruent with their aspirations. For instance, if you had a new, stylish property aiming for the discriminating individual traveller, such as lawyers, designers and architects you would be unwise to use Old English typeface in orange.

Name

The name of your hotel or restaurant is a very important part of how it is seen by your customers. However it is important to not get too hung up on names. The most important issue is not having anything that has negative connotations. Positive associations should flow over time from your quality service. Independent hotels often have names associated with their town, village or some other location and these usually serve very well. However, do consider the actual length of what you choose and the wisdom of including the word 'the' at the beginning and 'hotel' at the end. Your name needs to be recognisable quickly on signage, so short works better than long.

The difficulty comes when you are looking for a new name that does not have such an association or you are looking for a new name for your restaurant. It is becoming increasingly difficult to find new names that are legally available but whatever you choose, make sure that you check out the possibility of registration and the domain availability.

Colour

The choices that you make about colour are more important than you imagine. Often colour choices are made from a subjective point of view, with no reference to the market you are trying to reach. But because colour is energy, it affects our mood and influences our behaviour.

Angela Wright is a colour psychologist and she used to run a hotel. She realised that given a choice of two bedrooms that were identical in every way except the colour scheme regular guests would prefer one to the other. They were never able to explain their reasons except to say that they felt better when they were in a particular room. We underestimate the psychological impact of colour to our peril.

Research shows that people make subconscious judgements about people and products within 90 seconds of initial viewing. Between 60 per cent and 90 per cent of that judgement is based on colour alone. Over 90 per cent of consumers say they place most importance on visual factors (colour and shape) when purchasing a product, compared to only 6 per cent who say that the feel of the product is most important. For instance just a glimpse of the Coca-Cola bottle or its distinctive red is enough for us to recognise exactly what it is.

◆ TIP ◆

The use of the most appropriate colours for your hotel, whether it is in your décor or your literature, cannot be left to be the last decision. It is a fundamental part of projecting your vision and helps to differentiate you from the competition.

There are only eleven basic colour words in the English language and these colours have fundamental properties. For instance:

Red is a strong *physical* colour, lively and friendly, but can be seen as demanding and aggressive. It can make things appear nearer than they really are, so it grabs our attention.

Blue affects us *mentally*. Strong blues stimulate clear thought. It can appear to be cold, unemotional and unfriendly.

Yellow relates to the *emotions*, is the colour of confidence and optimism and lifts our spirits. The wrong tone can cause fear and anxiety.

Green is the colour of *balance* between body, mind and emotions and gives reassurance. It can be seen as too bland and indicate stagnation.

Angela Wright says of her hotel days, 'We quickly learned how to use colour. Blue never works in a restaurant. A little bit of red in the bar worked well. Green seemed to work pretty much anywhere. Too much yellow in a bedroom and you'd have bad-tempered guests.'

In looking at how colour is used in print or decoration it is not enough to just refer to blue or red, since there is no such thing as a universally attractive colour. It is the variations in each colour that are important since two variations of the same colour can have completely different effects. Our response is not to one colour but to colours in combination.

Angela Wright has developed the Colour Affects System (www.colour-affects.co.uk), which in summary seeks to describe four tonal families of colour. Each group contains variations of all the spectral hues, so for any colour scheme that you want to use in your hotel, whether in the literature or the furnishings, you only need to use one group. As you will see in the description above of the four primary colours, each colour has both negative and positive properties. Which of these are communicated depends entirely on how it is used.

Typography

It is not possible to have a coherent image for your hotel unless your use of typography has a unique personality. Although it seems a simple issue of 'just choosing a typeface', there are so many options for getting it wrong (font, size, alignment, spacing, shape, paragraphs etc) that you will soon recognise a page layout for a letter or a website that has been set up by an expert. You need to choose a serif (like the main text in this book) or sans serif (like that used in the headings) typeface or a combination of both and then make a selection based on the various sizes, weights and widths of the letters. You don't need to pay to have all your literature and signage set by a graphic designer each time. Far better to have a sample design template to use as a standard and then make sure that this is followed each time you produce a piece of print. The vital aspects of effective use of type are clarity and legibility.

Logo

A logotype is a set of words in a determined type font. Often it is used with a symbol that together forms a signature, as with say the BP logo. Legibility is imperative, as is its universal applicability on various different media, such as signs, letters and T-shirts.

Logos need to be distinctive but also durable. You do not want to spend time and effort being recognised only to change every few years. Indeed you won't find many large companies changing their logos very readily. How long do you think Ford have had their distinctive logo? You can use recognised typefaces or design something entirely new and individual. Whatever you use, it needs to express your positioning and your personality. The colours you use will also be an expression of the palette that you chose to represent your hotel.

Symbols

Symbols are used by the big brands to help differentiate themselves from their competition. These brand marks try to communicate the organisation's uniqueness in a split second. Think Nike, BMW, CNN or Michelin. Is there a place for symbols outside of the big brands? Personally I doubt that it is really worth the effort. These symbols are shorthand, used where there is little opportunity to say very much. They gain currency by being exposed on TV, billboards and in direct mail. We start to recognise the symbol because we see it so often.

In the case of a small business, there is not the marketing or media spend to make any symbol become that recognisable and in most case you have the opportunity to put the full logo anyway. If you have a crest or other design that works well with your logo then fine, but look at the balance within the whole signature to make sure that your main message comes across. I wouldn't recommend spending money on developing a new symbol.

Taglines

A tagline (or slogan) is a short phrase that captures a company's brand essence, personality and positioning and distinguishes it from the competition. If you think of Nike you associate the company with 'Just do it'. In the UK, the Malmaison group have used 'Hotels that dare to be different'. It is not imperative that you develop a slogan, although it can become a shorthand expression of what you are about. Something may develop from an exploration of your vision but don't just have a slogan for the sake of it. It needs to grow out of what you are actually about.

Paper

Your use of certain types of paper or card are again an expression of what you are trying to achieve with your target market. For instance using a piece of flimsy 80gsm paper will not be a very good advertisement for a gourmet dinner at £55 per person. Appropriateness is the key: if you have an up-market restaurant or hotel then your choice of paper for the menu or the brochure itself needs to reflect the hotel quality. But don't go over the top. Look at the competition and see where you fit. Brochures that are 12 pages and have tissue paper interleaves might give a misleading impression about your great value budget hotel.

Wording

Every hotel has to develop its own personality and the words you use reflect this. If your personality is an essential part of the service delivery then the 'voice' that comes across has to be yours. Whenever you write a letter or copy for a brochure try to keep it simple and direct. If your product is a bit alternative then it would make sense to maybe use an alternative copy style. Humour is always interesting but can be a little aggravating if you try too hard. Quirky works well if it is done well, but only if it reflects you and your hotel.

Consistency

Good design is good business, so it is vital that the whole issue of how your customers perceive you and your staff is given the amount of thought it deserves. You need to be consistent in all your communications so that you start to build up the value of all your efforts and expenditure. For instance your recruitment adverts need to have the same style as your advertisements for conferences and meetings. Any and every communication from you needs to be instantly recognisable as being from you, either in the consistent use of your colour or the way that the words are laid out.

Although it seems to be very pedantic, you need to value your corporate identity in the same way that you value any other asset. Over time you will spend a lot of money making it valuable, so it is wise to look after and nurture it. Make sure that you use your agreed logo in the same way every time it is reproduced. Always check the colours and the typeface.

Outside

As I said earlier, I see many hotels that really let themselves down by how they look from the road. If I see a broken sign or weeds growing in the car park it doesn't give me much encouragement about the care that the hotel is likely to offer to guests. Of course I may be wrong, and the gardener has it on his list for tomorrow, but can you afford to take the risk that I might drive by?

On the other hand I may not be your target market, so it is all a question of congruence. If your target audience care about standards then you need to make sure that your standards meet their expectations. The trick is to keep looking at your physical product as if you are seeing it for the first time, which is difficult. One solution is to make a checklist and make sure that someone checks it at least every week.

◆ **TIP** ◆

The outside is what people see before they ever see your bedrooms, meeting rooms or restaurant. If the outside puts them off then they will never know what your rooms are like.

If you have limited funds for development, it may be more profitable to spend it on the outside rather than the inside. At least if you can entice people inside, you have the chance to work your charm on them.

Signage

Signage is probably one of the most important but often most neglected aspects of your physical product. How many people see it depends on your road position, but even if it is only committed customers that see it, poor signage can undo all that good work that you have done to get your customer over the threshold. What your signs look like will be a development of the work that you have done on your logo and the colours that you have chosen.

There are many different types of signage products, from plastic to wood with much in between. Plastic suits fast food outlets, and traditional wooden signs suit traditional businesses, such as country house hotels. Keep the wording simple and to the point and make sure that these words are readable from the road.

Remember that your customers and guests tend to lose the use of part of their brain when they are in 'foreign' territory: I know I do whenever I go to an airport. Walk through the whole journey from car park to bedrooms and in reverse and wherever there is a choice of where to go, put a direction sign.

Inside

The same issues apply to the inside of your property. Does it always reflect exactly the image that you want to give? Have you allowed some very cheap signs to be stuck up around the building to promote a special night in the restaurant or bar? Although you might have got used to them, any new customer might be negatively surprised by their cheap quality. It is the same with how a room smells: you may have got used to that stale smell, but will it be the first thing a potential customer notices? Check that all areas are comfortable; some sofas look great but give you backache.

For some reason operators of hotels tend to be very unresponsive to the atmosphere in their property. The lighting is often very harsh and the music off or too quiet. Ambience needs to be created instantly and you cannot wait even an hour to change it. If your restaurant is quiet then dim the lights, put some candles on the tables and turn the music up. The same goes for reception areas, which often look like station concourses. Every location within your building needs to be constantly monitored and changes made to reflect the needs of the moment.

It is easy to get used to things yourself, so you need to continually ask new people to assess you. This is where mystery shopping can be a great help, but if you use an outside company brief them carefully on your operational standards so that they know what to measure.

It is also vital that you have an overall colour scheme for the interior. You will probably carry out redecoration over a long period so it is easy to introduce different colour schemes without really thinking about it. Choose a colour palette and stick to it. (See page 6.)

People

I do not intend to cover customer service in this book, but you need to be aware of the impact that your staff have on the way that your hotel is perceived. They are often seen as the product, since they are the ones that deliver the service. So what they look like is very important, not only in the clothes or uniforms they wear but also their general demeanour. Do they have a genuine and ready smile (one that involves their mouth *and* their eyes) and are they always on the look out for ways to help?

You cannot help but be impressed by the results achieved by

Ritz-Carlton Hotels who have surveyed their guests and found that 80 per cent were 'extremely satisfied'. Their customer service delivery is based on 250 hours training in the first year, using a fairly simple approach:

- A warm and sincere greeting.
- Using the customer's name if possible.
- A constant anticipation of the customer's needs.
- A warm goodbye, using the customer's name if possible.

DOES YOUR PRODUCT SUIT THE MARKET?

Ensuring that your hotel meets the needs of your customers is a continuous exercise, although it can be a bit of a chicken and egg situation; you know who your current customers are and you can talk to them, but what about the customers you don't have? What product features could you develop that would attract them? How can you really find out the potential for a new spa facility? Whatever the scale of your operation, delivering the totality of the hotel product is a complex operation. For instance the seemingly simple provision of room service has wide-ranging implications that involve service, both to the room and afterwards, physical things like trays and hot cupboards as well as considerations about the facility to eat a meal in the room.

It is therefore useful to consider your total hotel product as being made up of three components, which all need separate consideration:

1 **Service:** Issues such as friendliness, speed, attitude and professionalism.

2 **Environment**: Issues such as design, décor, comfort, ambience and atmosphere.

3 **Physical aspects:** Issues such as room size, beds, lighting, temperature control, bathrooms, DVDs, internet access and desks.

Product research

It is important that you continuously ask your customers what they think of what you offer. You need to set up a system for collecting and analysing feedback from your customers. This can just be a questionnaire in the rooms or on the tables in the restaurant, although these often give a distorted view. People are naturally less inclined to give positive feedback and you will have a higher proportion of negative comments. Just think how many of these forms you complete yourself when you are out.

Far better to have a proactive system for generating feedback: for overnight guests you probably have their e-mail address so after they check out send them an online questionnaire. Don't make it too long – up to 10 questions should be OK. (There is more information on the measurement of customer satisfaction in Chapter 10.)

Also consider the views of meeting planners and corporate bookers. They will have good insight into how you rate against the other facilities that they use. If anyone comes up with really interesting ideas call him or her and try to provoke an in-depth discussion.

If you are launching a new hotel then research again is a key activity. Open your mind to the endless possibilities of making a product that is exciting and unusual; continually surprise your guests and they will tell their friends. To stand out from the crowd be a bit quirky or maybe develop a theme that suits your temperament, whether that is music, art, walking, racing or sailing. This way you can laser-target your marketing and attract guests with lots of tailor-made packages and find local partners willing to co-promote with you.

Keep evolving

No market stays still for very long. Customers' needs and attitudes change and you have to respond. Think about the attitude to smoking and how this has affected the way that you present your room product. Food service has undergone a mini-revolution, forcing all traditional hotels to be very creative about their restaurant offer.

The development of boutique hotels is a particularly interesting phenomenon. They were developed by entrepreneurial individuals as a counterpoint to the formulaic offering from the large groups and were successful maybe because of their design influence, but mostly because they met the needs of a more independent, design conscious traveller. Now that the large groups are developing boutique hotels, will there continue to be the same attraction to the original independent traveller who had 'discovered' something new and different?

Room product

Technology has also had a big impact on all areas of your business. Corporate guests are now demanding broadband and

WiFi as well as better in-room entertainment with more TV channels and DVD players. Whatever facilities you have it is vital that your staff have at least a rudimentary knowledge of how things work; no client wants to be told to wait until your IT specialist is available in the morning to sort out his laptop. If you provide meeting rooms you need to be prepared for meeting organisers bringing in all sorts of technical equipment.

You need also to consider the different habits of your male and female business travellers. Women tend to treat their room as a home away from home and will often spend the evening in their rooms; they appreciate a bath and a good room service meal. Men on the other hand will often go to your bar and restaurant after their workday finishes.

Whatever your product, whether you are a small hotel in the country or a larger property in a city centre, the demands of your customer are changing all the time. You need to be aware of the trends and decide whether it is profitable for you to change your offer. Sometimes because of your competitive situation you just cannot afford not to change. Be very critical about every thing you do and evaluate your service and facilities. Don't do things just because it has always been that way. Be prepared to innovate: consider, amongst others things, your bathroom amenities, irons and ironing boards, door security features, safes, CD/DVD players and 24-hour snack facilities.

However don't innovate just for the sake of it and don't introduce amenities as an alternative to real hospitality. Many chain properties, and others too, continually add pillows, cushions and throws to the bedroom. This is maybe what they think the customer wants, but it has a big implication for the time it takes to clean the room. As an alternative, I am sure that your guest would rather have a really sincere welcome from the owner/manager. Some of the best ideas come from your team, so don't leave them out of the feedback loop.

◆ **TIP** ◆

In your search for the future don't forget the basics. Sometimes it is easy to add a DVD player but not monitor the quality of the mattresses. The fundamental service that you provide is a good night's sleep; so put all your efforts into creating this experience.

You are the most appropriate person to check your given experience. Spend the night in a range of your own rooms and consider:

◆ What can you hear through the walls and the windows?

◆ Is the room clean, with no stains, chipped paint or peeling paper?

◆ Does the lighting suit the tasks (reading and writing)?

◆ Is the furniture in good condition?

◆ Is the TV reception acceptable, can you see the picture from the bed and a chair and does the handset work?

◆ Do the heating and air conditioning work effectively?

◆ Is the bed comfortable, without dips in the middle of the mattress?

◆ Does the room smell fresh?

- Is the bathroom spotless, with good ventilation and no mould around the tub or shower?

- Does the shower head have lime scale, or leak?

- If you have a safe can you read the instructions easily?

- Can you see the alarm clock from the bed?

- Are the desk space and the chair user friendly?

- Are there enough power outlets and in the right place?

- What difficulties are there for overseas guests particularly those who don't have English as their first language?

I am sure you can think of other items to check. If you are not 100 per cent satisfied then neither will your guest be. With all the competition from franchises and chains you cannot afford to forget the basics.

Restaurant offer

Deciding on the best strategy for a hotel restaurant offer is often a very difficult decision. If you operate a hotel that has more of a pub offering then it is easier to integrate the restaurant into the community. A traditional hotel seems to create barriers that are difficult to overcome. Sometimes you are constrained by other parts of your business; bookers of weddings seem to expect that you operate a full à la carte restaurant.

There is no one particular answer to the dilemma but what is certain is that there is very rarely any place for a hotel restaurant serving 'a range of international dishes'. Essentially the more you can make your restaurant like an independent outlet the better, and that includes recruiting restaurant, rather than hotel, staff to run it. If you have a separate entrance then you definitely have a greater chance of making a success.

One strategy is to look for specific types of cuisine that are not offered in your area, whether this is Italian, Thai or even Russian! If you combine this with an effective campaign to entice local patronage as well as use by your hotel guests you will at least have a chance of making it a success. Again research is the key, although this too has its limitations, since you have to decide the difference between a fad and a trend. Nevertheless customers are now much better educated about food and do appreciate well-prepared local ingredients at great value for money.

There are a few other options for food service in your hotel. City centre hotels can avoid providing a full restaurant service altogether so long as there is a good range of local offerings. You could benefit from leasing your premises to a chef who is keen to have his own business but has no capital or backing. The only thing you then have to decide is who provides breakfast. Depending on your location your restaurant space may be of interest to a national franchise, particularly one that provides all-day service.

On the other hand a city centre location gives you access to a great many potential customers. In the midst of some very disappointing offerings in London, The Goring Hotel's redesigned restaurant has shown what can be done if you put in a great deal of thought and effort.

Profitability

The key to understanding the importance of each of the different elements of your product is to analyse their individual contribution and/or profitability. You need this information so that you can plan where to allocate your effort and your promotional expenditure.

The hotel business is no different from a lot of others where most of your profit comes from identifiable days or customers. It can be helpful to use the Pareto principle, which says that 80 per cent of your outcomes will come from 20 per cent of your effort. This is the background to the 80/20 rule that looks at sales and profits and identifies the largest sources of contribution. These are not precise figures but they will help identify the source of the majority of the activity being measured. For instance most restaurants make most (80 per cent) of their profit on a Friday and a Saturday (2 days out of 7 or 28 per cent), which give 80/28 profit to effort.

You should consider analysing:

- menu item sales volume;
- total sales (room nights) per corporate client;
- meeting spend per customer;
- average rate per channel (direct/wholesaler/third parties);
- profitability per department (rooms/F&B/leisure).

To work out the proportions you need to:

1 Calculate the profit or sales contributed by each of these activities over a given period and add for a total. Make sure the period is representative and not seasonal.

2 Arrange the values in descending order.

3 Calculate the value of each activity as a percentage of the total for the period.

4 Calculate the cumulative percentage in descending order.

5 Find the row where the cumulative percentage is near to 80 per cent cumulative. Then read across to see what proportion of activities accounts for this 80 per cent. For example, only 10 clients might account for 80 per cent of your corporate room nights and you actually have 40 clients. The ratio is therefore 80/25.

This does not mean that you should ignore the other 75 per cent of your customers! However you should probably review these customers and see if, with some effort, you could develop them into more productive users.

Segmentation

Whatever your product, it will not appeal to the whole of the hotel using market. For instance, just by charging a different price to the hotel down the road you have segmented your market by price. The challenge is to establish segments of customers who have the same needs and therefore act similarly in response to your offer.

Classification

From this you can see that defining your customers in terms of socio-economics (e.g. ABC1 etc), demographics (e.g. men aged 20–35) and geo-demographics (e.g. everyone in the same street) is not really segmentation at all but classification. This classification is not very helpful in marketing terms since the needs of people in the same classification will be entirely different. Two neighbours in the same street may want completely different things from a restaurant; for instance one wanting value for money and the other prepared to pay an above average price if the restaurant is the latest place to go.

Psychographics

From time to time different organisations come up with ready-made segment descriptors that have gone some way to define groups with the same needs. We all remember the Yuppies, the Baby Boomers, Empty Nesters and now there are Generation Y and the Silver Surfers.

Their common attitudes, needs, opinions and lifestyle behaviour may be appropriate to your product but you need to find groups of prospects that you can actually reach, and where the lifestyle variables don't overlap. This is not an easy thing to do. Ideally you would go through a process where you define your market, find out what motivates your customers, group these customers together in clusters, establish segments and then test your assumptions to see if the segment is viable in terms of access and distinctiveness.

Reality

Often the only real segmentation practised within most hotels is one of 'purpose of travel' (and this is certainly better than nothing!). Daily statistics are usually kept that differentiate guests as staying for *business* (sometimes broken down further into individuals, corporate accounts and meetings) or for *leisure* (sometimes broken down into individuals, groups and special promotions).

A useful segmentation that can tie in with your other promotional activity is to look at benefit segments. Once you have isolated all your benefits from your list of features (see 'How does the competition compare? on pages 30–35) you will see that there are different groups of guests that respond to different benefits, depending on their purpose for travel and also other factors. It is reasonable therefore to assume that it is possible to predict buying behaviour from the different benefits that are sought. For instance, think of any fast food outlet and you will appreciate that the only segmentation that is evident is that of the benefits of 'quick' and 'cheap'.

Differentiating

To effectively market your hotel you need to get your offer right by differentiating your product to appeal to specific segments.

◆ TIP ◆

To define your segment you need to focus on your market by thinking, 'Our market is those people who want ...'.

For instance, your result could be 'our leisure market is those people who are nostalgic for old-fashioned hospitality and appreciate home-cooked food'. To implement this strategy you would ensure that your physical product met these needs and you could isolate the segment by the way that your internet site text was written and the keywords that you used for the search criteria.

If you just want more of the segment of customers that you already have you can use them as your research sample. You will already have some idea of why they use your hotel and you can try to find out in detail exactly what they consider to be their main motivators for using your hotel. Use some of the same techniques that are described in Chapter 10 under 'How to measure customer satisfaction'.

Positioning

Positioning, often referred to as branding, is about creating an image in your customers' minds. If you understand your target market then you can match their needs and desires with the image that you want to create. Actually having your hotel perceived by your customers exactly as you would wish it is very difficult. The brand image or position is what the customer perceives; it is those attributes that exist only in the mind of the consumer.

To differentiate your hotel from all the others in your competitive set you have to market the intangible elements of your operation. The problem is that most hotels stick to the things that they can see (the tangible elements) and try and promote their hotel by showing pictures of the outside of the building or of empty hotel rooms. All this does is lead to sameness and selling on price, with the hotel stay reduced to just another commodity, not a rewarding emotional experience. You will have heard the entreaty 'Sell the sizzle, not the steak!' All steaks (by and large) are the same, so to differentiate your restaurant you need to sell the sizzle. It is only by somehow making this sizzle tangible that you can position your hotel as being different to the competition.

Effective positioning not only creates an image but also makes a promise through a range of benefits that your customer will receive. It needs to offer a solution to a perceived problem. A good positioning statement can be very powerful: Avis Car Rental – We Try Harder. Your positioning strategy is at the heart of your operation and affects everything that you do – advertising, promotions, brochures, facilities, customer relations and everything else that adds up to the hospitality experience. Your positioning is therefore part of your vision.

Unique selling proposition (USP)

It is worth mentioning the concept of the USP, since much literature maintains that every organisation needs one! In some ways this is true, but having set out your *vision* and established your *position* you have already well prepared yourself to slay the competition.

It was Rosser Reeves, Chairman of advertising agency Ted Bates, who first formulated the concept of a Unique Selling Proposition in his book *Reality of Advertising* (1961). He was only articulating what had been the practice since packaged goods had started to be distributed and slogans had been used to promote the products.

The concept may not be as useful today as it was, particularly with the advent of sophisticated global brands. Indeed Wally Olins in his book *On Brand* calls the concept 'pseudo-scientific nonsense'. In a way he is right, particularly if a USP is taken in isolation from the vision or brand experience; but if it helps to isolate some key benefits of particular services in your hotel then that must be beneficial. The limitation of the traditional USP is that it can help generate a proposition that is unique but it does not necessarily fully position your product. A USP is a set of words, which don't always fully articulate your vision.

Features and benefits

Every hotel is made up of a range of products and services and you will be able to list all the features of your hotel. But customers and guests do not buy features; they buy the benefits that they gain from the features. To isolate your benefits you first need to list your features; include all your technical characteristics, services, prices and quality. You need to differentiate between each of your specific market opportunities: rooms/meeting rooms/restaurant/bar/leisure etc. because certain features will have different benefits depending on the market segment you are serving.

◆ TIP ◆

A feature describes what your service or product does while a benefit describes what customer need it fulfils.

A simple way to isolate the benefit from each feature is to ask the question 'Which means that ...?' For instance if you have tea and coffee making facilities it means that guests can have a hot drink whenever they like, without leaving their room or waiting for room service.

Of course not all benefits are as important as each other, and you can only find this out by asking your customers. Some benefits will not be significant differentiators from the competition and you need to isolate those benefits that are either unique to you or not used by any of your competition.

The benefits depend on the target market and each feature needs to be carefully analysed for each particular segment. For instance, near my home there is a really great little country house hotel that has a resident hawker with about 30 of these birds. He gives demonstrations and keeps some birds on the lawn. This is a really interesting feature but for the majority of that hotel's customers it is not an important benefit.

Here are some hotel features that have been converted to benefits from the point of view of the business user:

Features	Benefits
Old hotel	There is a sense of history.
New hotel	All the facilities are new and up to date.
Large hotel	There is plenty of room for large meetings.
Small hotel	We know each guest by name.
Large gardens	You can relax and walk to your heart's content.
Large rooms	There is plenty of space in which to work and relax.
King size beds	You can relax and not feel cramped.
Gym	You can work out after a hard day at work.
Spa	Relax and feel pampered after a hard day at work.
Range of conference rooms	We can cope with changes to numbers for your meeting.
24-hour reception	We can respond to any request at any time of the day.

Restaurant	You don't have to leave the hotel to go in search of food.
Bar	You can have a drink with your colleagues after normal closing time.

HOW DOES THE COMPETITION COMPARE?

No one operates any sort of accommodation business in isolation. Even if you are the only hotel on a remote island with no local competition, you are nevertheless competing with other islands, however far away. Customers and guests always have a choice.

It is vital that you take the time to investigate where you fit into the local range of options available to corporate users, leisure guests and meeting planners. This knowledge about your existing direct competition and any new ones will enable you to:

- evaluate your own performance;
- identify and exploit competitor's weaknesses;
- combat competitor strengths;
- get new ideas;
- maybe identify new prospects.

There is really no need to be scared of this activity. It doesn't involve anything illegal: you won't need to put on a black polo-neck jumper and get involved in breaking and entering! Most of the information you need is freely and legally available.

One of the key benefits of any systematic competitor evaluation is the buy-in from the team. I recommend that as many people as possible are involved – receptionists, chefs, housekeepers. You should include overnight stays with simple feedback reports at the end. You can really boost the willingness of receptionists and reservation specialists to go for rate maximisation after they have seen the competition.

Benchmarking

This is a slightly different evaluation, which can be used in a couple of different ways.

1 **Reference**: You can choose a hotel on which you would like to model your offer, as a sort of reference point. This does not have to be any competition to you and could even be in another country. You choose it because you consider that its offer will suit your local market. (Be careful about importing services and facilities without checking their local applicability and the costs.)

2 **Evaluating**: The other use for benchmarking is in evaluating your business performance. You can check your occupancy and average rate against your local colleagues or a national average. You can also look at food and beverage margins or staff turnover against industry norms.

Another benchmark is the 'Common Accommodation Standards', which will apply to all providers of accommodation in Britain from January 2008. These standards will replace the current star and diamond systems administered by the different organisations. They have been agreed by VisitBritain, VisitScotland, the Wales Tourist Board, the AA and the RAC to help customers understand the quality rating given to particular establishments. Any move to reduce confusion must be a move in the right direction but with five categories of 'hotel' and five categories of 'guest accommodation', it may take the consumer some time to understand the benchmarks and be able to compare one establishment with another.

Your competition is likely to be from those establishments in the same categories and the same start rating but this may not always be the case. Your local knowledge and feedback from clients will tell you your real competition.

Who are your competitors?

These will generally be properties that are also supplying or have the opportunity to supply your current customers. The most important consideration here is that you will be competing with different hotels depending on your different facilities. For instance a hotel that you compete with for corporate business may well not be competition for your meeting facilities. Be realistic about the number of hotels you choose for each of your segments (rooms/meting rooms/restaurants/leisure) and choose no more than five.

What is their offer?

Check your competition's total offer in the segment that you have decided is competitive. Look at how their service and facilities compare with yours and make sure that you follow the whole experience from start to finish. Check how long they take to respond to an e-mail or a telephone request for information. Are there any aspects of competitive service that you could usefully incorporate?

What are their prices and rates?

This is the start of your evaluation of comparative values. Once you have a summary of their facilities, their prices and rates you can consider whether you think customers will pay more or less for *your* offer. Does your room product justify an extra £10 compared to the competition?

Who are their customers?

This information is sometimes difficult to gain. Nevertheless you will probably find that many of your customers are also customers for your competition. Sometimes it is common knowledge when there are a number of large corporate accounts in an area. You can also check their meetings boards to see who is using the meeting rooms, but don't forget to wear a hat and a false beard!

How do they promote themselves?

Do they do anything different to you? Do they have a specialist sales executive? Find out everything you can about how they reach their market including their memberships of representation organisations.

How are they organised?

Much of your local competition will be organised in a very different way to you. They could have similar ownership but with a manager, or they could be part of a chain or franchise. All this is very useful information. Find out how many staff they employ and what their turnover is. Maybe some of your staff now work there or vice versa? What is the working atmosphere like?

What are their strengths and weaknesses?

You now need to make sense of all this information. Listing strengths and weaknesses is a good way to summarise information into a usable form. List what they are good at and how it compares with you. Focus on how they meet customer needs and the particular benefits they deliver.

Then list all the areas that they are less good at. Do these give you an opportunity to exploit? These summaries will help you evaluate your competitive edge.

How to gather the information

There are a wide variety of sources of competitive intelligence:

Common contacts

Contact anyone who also talks to your competitors:

- Customers: are they satisfied?
- Ex-employees: anything significant?
- Suppliers: what are they buying/investing in?
- Distributors: have they heard anything from users?

Industry

Make the most of any information they have given out:

- Associations: statements or comments made at local meetings.
- Interviews: maybe something in the local press?

Their own publicity

What they say about themselves:

- Press releases: details may be biased.
- Job advertisements: difficulty in keeping staff or maybe they are expanding?
- Marketing campaigns: what are they planning next?
- Websites: maybe something interesting announced in advance?

Intelligence gathering

This is not really espionage!

- Personal visits: make a good excuse to be a prospect.
- Leaks: you never know where they come from!

Counter intelligence

You could take the view that 'All's fair in love and war' and therefore not worry that your rivals are probably approaching your hotel on the same basis. However the market is tough and you don't want to give up any advantage unless you have to. The most secure organisation is one where the whole team is focused on the business objectives. If you make sure that all your sales procedures are in place and that you don't give out price information without a thorough investigation, at least you won't make your rivals' job very easy.

KEY POINTS

- Ensure that your product (rooms/restaurant/meeting rooms/leisure) continues to meet the needs of your market.
- Position your hotel in line with your stated vision.
- Make a list of hotel features and then list the different benefits for each of your major market segments.

- Maintain consistency in your corporate identity.

- Check the outside look of your hotel every day and encourage your team to also consider it their responsibility.

- Constantly monitor the atmosphere inside the hotel.

- Make sure that you and your team constantly check the competition and report back.

2

Where Do You Want To Be?

Before considering the customers you can attract and the channels to reach them, it is vital to articulate your vision of what sort of accommodation business you are trying to be.

WHAT IS YOUR VISION FOR THE FUTURE?

Can you recall why you came into the accommodation business in the first place and what you expected to achieve? If you ever thought that it was an easy way to make a lot of money for very little work you have probably found out the hard way already that it's not. It is a business where service is delivered to people by people, whether you call them staff and customers or team members and guests. As Rick Stein says, 'We're in this business to entertain people, not make our own lives easy.'

When I talk about vision I do not mean 'Do you have a mission statement?' These tend to be very bland and generic statements that could apply to any hotel including your competition. They are so short as to be meaningless and set down by management as a guide to behaviour. Often they cause more amusement than commitment, especially if they talk about work/life balance in an organisation where managers have to work over 60 hours a week! You cannot graft a mission statement on to an organisation that has been set up just to make a profit and then sit back and think that your team will be happy and contented as you exploit them. Many of us have worked for companies that talk about 'people being our greatest asset' while the chairman swans off to the Caribbean in his yacht for two months but won't pay double time at Christmas!

A vision is much more than a mission statement. It is the glue that keeps the organisation together, it is the reason that you do what you do and it is what drives you to get up in the morning.

Your vision encompasses all that you imagine your business to be, from the service to the staff and from the customers to the environment.

The best businesses to work in are developed by individuals who have the ability to imagine what others cannot see and the tenacity to deliver what they believe is possible: you need to be able to articulate your vision so that everyone can buy into it. Visions, just like problems, are much better if they are shared!

Companies such as Sony, Nike, and Caterpillar have great brands and are good examples of consistency, but these are corporate entities that have travelled a long way from their founders' original vision. There are a few examples of large corporations that have still managed to be identified with a personality and a vision, such as Virgin with Richard Branson and Body Shop with Anita Roddick. In the hotel sector you cannot help but be impressed by the vision of Ken McCulloch and his Malmaison, Columbus and Dakota Hotels.

Virgin

Richard Branson started his entrepreneurial career while still at school. Academic studies were not his strong point and his mail order record business soon became a shop. Virgin Records was formed in 1972, named for the fact that this was his first venture. Branson's vision is to challenge the way things are traditionally done. He finds areas of business that are done badly or where the customer has been ripped off and goes into that business with the express idea of shaking it up (let's hope that his experiment with trains has a happy outcome).

His vision is to challenge the status quo and at the same time he has a view about how people work best. He knows he is not always the expert, so he sets up joint ventures and he develops independent companies (40 at the last count) where the scale of the operation does not dwarf the enterprise. His values permeate the whole Virgin group:

- ◆ Value for money – not necessarily the cheapest but simple, honest and transparent pricing.

- ◆ Good quality – always deliver on promises with great attention to detail.

- Brilliant customer service – professional but uncorporate, friendly, human and relaxed.
- Innovative – challenging conventional service ideas and using stylish design.
- Competitively challenging – fighting the big boys by gaining public sympathy for the 'underdog'.
- Fun – always trying to give customers entertainment and making Virgin a fun place to work.

In essence he has a very simple business philosophy. If you recruit the right people, treat them well and trust them you will have happy customers and consequently profits. Maybe it is as simple as this?

The Body Shop

Anita Roddick and her husband originally opened a restaurant and a hotel in her hometown. When he wanted to trek across the Americas, she needed to provide an income for the family. During her own extensive travels she had noticed lots of different body rituals practised by women around the world. This led directly to the first Body Shop in 1976. Since then the shops have expanded across the globe and there are now nearly 2,000 shops in 50 different markets. Despite conflicts between the need to make money and her principles, and the occasional bad patch, the shops have flourished and she has managed not to compromise her original vision to effect social and environmental change.

As anyone who has shopped at The Body Shop knows, their principles are well articulated and you either buy into their vision or not – it is your choice. Their values:

◆ Against animal testing – they consider testing ingredients on animals to be morally and scientifically indefensible.

◆ Support community trade – they support small producer communities around the world.

◆ Activate self-esteem – they treat everyone as an individual.

◆ Defend human rights – they believe that it is everyone's responsibility to actively support those whose rights are denied to them.

◆ Protect the planet – they believe that businesses have a responsibility to protect the environment in which they operate.

Many companies have tried to reproduce the products and bring them to market at lower prices. Despite this competition, the organisation still endures.

The takeover by L'Oreal would not seem to be an obvious move. However, it will be fascinating to see how much the unique values of Body Shop influence the operation of L'Oreal itself.

Ken McCulloch

After his success with One Devonshire Gardens in Glasgow, Ken McCulloch developed the Malmaison group of hotels in the UK. He eventually sold the company to a group, then went on to develop the first Columbus Hotel in Monaco and has recently opened the first Dakota Hotel. His hospitality vision seems to have gestated a bit like Richard Branson's as a counterbalance to the terrible operations perpetrated by the 'big boys' – he says, 'We will always be a wee company that thinks big.'

He always seems to be fighting the 'What do they expect for £80' school of hotel keeping, striving all the time to make his guests' stay a memorable experience rather than a chore. There is no doubt that he has been extremely successful in generating great occupancy levels and above average room rates. He too makes his pricing transparent and fair, giving tremendous value for money especially compared to his perceived competition. McCulloch's vision can be summarised as:

- Always go with your instincts and trust the public.
- Simple pricing drives loyalty.
- Never compromise on quality and design standards.
- Always strive to impress your guests.
- Turn employees into believers.
- Try to make it the friendliest hotel guests have ever stayed in.
- A great restaurant is the heart and soul of the hotel.
- Make guests look forward to being away.
- Think about the language and humour you use to communicate.
- Guests want to be 'wowed' and they don't care how.
- Always share your vision with your people.

Articulate your vision

I have used these three examples to illustrate what I mean by having a vision and articulating it. This vision then becomes what drives your business and is the backdrop to every decision you make for your hotel. Think of it as being something that you need so that you can talk about it to any applicant for a job in your hotel. Just a simple piece of A4 will do but it needs to summarise exactly what you are trying to do. Applicants can then see what is expected of them and they can decide whether or not it's for them.

Here are a few ideas of what you should consider as you try to set down your vision for your hotel. You don't even have to write very much. Some organisations just set down their vision as a picture. It doesn't matter, since there is no format or right way of expressing what you 'see'. But you must be able to communicate it.

Staff
What do you expect from your team?
How do you organise decision-making?
How empowered are the individuals?
What is your policy on skills development?

Food
What are you trying to achieve with your food?
Do you have a strict policy on local or organic produce?

Work ethic
What is your own attitude to working in the business?
How do you help with a good work/life balance?

Atmosphere
How do you want your guests to feel?
What sort of environment do you want to create for customers and staff?

Participation
What incentives do you have in place?
How do you share the profits?
How do staff participate in decision-making?

Colours
In what colours do you visualise your hotel?

Pictures
Are there any pictures that summarise what you 'see'?
What other hotels have you seen that you would like to emulate?

Markets
What market segments is your hotel trying to satisfy?

Communication
How do you organise communication?
Is communication really two-way?

Value proposition
What is your pricing policy?
How are you going to construct your value for money proposition?

I am sure that you can combine some of the aspects from the examples above and add your own ingredients, so that you can have an answer to the question, 'What is your vision for this hotel?'

WHAT TYPES OF CUSTOMER ARE AVAILABLE?

There are hundreds of opportunities to fill your rooms and your meeting facilities. The only limitation is your imagination and the scope of your individual facilities. If you only have five rooms and there is good regular demand from some local businesses, some of the opportunities highlighted here may not be very interesting. Indeed many of these opportunities are created by your proximity to the facilities concerned. For instance if the nearest university is over half an hour's drive away your potential from that source will be limited.

Make a note of anything you think might work and see what techniques you may be able to use to attract the business. Business often comes from the most unexpected source, so cast your net very wide before you home in on the real potential.

Note that there are different sources for the same type of business and it is sometimes a complicated chain. For example, a business traveller might make a booking via a travel agent who accesses the GDS (Global Distribution System, see page 70), with the reservation then being delivered to you by your representative organisation. This is still a company booking, with the travel agent being the source and the GDS and your representative being the technology.

Below are the various types of business that are available to all hotels. How many are available to you will depend on your location and facilities.

Airline crew

If your hotel is located near an airport you have the opportunity to accommodate airline crews. Generally airlines try to schedule their flights so that crew do not have to be away from home, but sometimes there is a very early flight that necessitates an overnight stop. An airline will make a long-term contract for a certain number of rooms each day, often over weekends and in the peak and the off-peak season. If an airline contract will not be more than 20 per cent of your total room count then it is good business to have. Because of the perceived benefit to the hotel the room rate is generally very low, often around 50 per cent of your headline rate, although this depends on the local supply situation.

The most difficult equation is the amount of business that you will displace by having a crew. You need to balance definite revenue (at a low average room rate) against your expectations (probably at a higher rate) and also take into account the fact that airline crew do not add much to your food and beverage revenue.

Crew are also very demanding guests, often needing to sleep during the day and checking in and out at strange times. You will need to rearrange your cleaning schedules and alter some administration procedures.

The first point of contact is the local station manager, to find out the local need and the timing of the contract negotiation. Very often a committee made up of a union representative, the local manager and the crew manager from head office makes the decisions.

Associations

Association meetings can be national, regional or international, and they can be booked anything up to ten years in advance. Generally the meeting has to be invited to a specific city by a local organisation and you might well be involved with this organisation through your local hotel association. However, these meetings often have a large number of delegates and need to take place in a non-hotel facility.

The potential for a hotel in these circumstances is in accommodating overnight visitors to the meeting. You need to be wary of allocating a large proportion of your rooms to the organising committee, particularly if there is a large proportion of the available hotel supply located between your hotel and the venue. Not only is it likely that there will be significant cancellations for the less prime locations as the date gets close, but also you may have to guarantee your prices. Sometimes it is more profitable to pick up individuals displaced by the visiting meeting delegates.

If the reservations are not made centrally then you may be able to get a list of delegates from the Association or from their appointed organiser for your own individual follow up.

Charities

Charities generally do not have much money to spend on meetings and accommodation. However they do need to get their staff and volunteers together from time to time. You will have times during the year when you know you are going to have weak demand both for meeting rooms and for bedrooms. These dates may coincide with the needs of particular charities but in any case you will find that they are more flexible than other organisers. Decide on your best rate and approach the charities direct. Start with any that have a local association, since they will probably be responsible for any regional meetings.

Coach companies

Coaches company work both on their own account and also on contract to larger group operators. They can be a direct source of business for hotels that have at least 25 rooms; those that can accommodate a coach-full. Many coach companies arrange their own tours, from their home base mostly, naturally enough to tourist destinations. They also arrange one-off trips to concerts, sports events and country houses and gardens.

If you feel that there is potential for your hotel, you have the space and the rate that you can achieve seems attractive, you can propose a joint venture with the coach company. Sharing the advertising costs makes you a partner rather than a supplier and puts you in a stronger position. To reach these companies you can purchase a list and make direct contact but one of the best ways to see if there is potential is to look out for any coaches in your area and then phone the number on the back of the coach.

Rates tend to be low but for a corporate hotel that would otherwise be empty over a holiday period, the room revenue plus the incremental spend can be very helpful. Operators usually ask for one free place per 20 passengers, which usually works out as two single rooms for the driver and escort in return for a full coach load of around 50 passengers.

Companies/organisations

For many hotels the weekly pattern will be business travellers Monday to Thursday and leisure travellers Friday to Sunday. The relative demand will dictate your room yield, since the weekend demand may well be higher than the corporate demand. If you are in an isolated rural location then demand will be limited to travellers stopping off en route from one place to another. Room demand will generally be for single use, preferably of a double room. If the likely visitors are contractors, then they may well be interested in twin rooms, to keep their costs down.

Whatever you do be consistent. Pitch your rates at the target market with the greatest potential, taking into account the style and service of your hotel but also the other guests. Don't target one market and then give up when things are not going to expectation and drop your rates to fill up with say contactors, who often try for four to a room to keep the costs really low! All this will do is drive away the business that you do have and you will have to start all over again.

Organisations generate both individuals as well as groups, although many of these groups are associated with overnight meetings.

Direct
Gaining both individual and group business from local companies depends on your local relationships. You need to find out who is the decision maker (probably a local contact but it can be the travellers themselves) and do some research to find out what is the potential and how the reservations are made by each different organisation. It is likely that you will need to 'steal' business from another hotel and this can take time and ingenuity.

Once you have worked out how much potential revenue can be gained from a particular company over one or two years you will be able to decide how much effort and money to put into soliciting the business. You can entertain decision makers individually or in small groups at your hotel but if the potential is large enough and there are a large number of companies you can also plan some 'open' days, to show off your talents.

To gain direct business from companies that are not local is quite difficult, since the decision makers are hard to find. Exposure on third party websites does give you the national exposure that you need. It may also be sensible to join a marketing consortium that puts some effort into reaching potential individual national and international travellers.

> If your meeting and conference facilities are extensive, it can be a good idea to take space at an exhibition, either a national or a local one. You can take space on your own or as part of a consortium that could be put together by your local chamber or business group.

Through travel agents including in-plants

Many companies have such a large travel requirement that they appoint a travel agent to either operate from their office (an in-plant) or manage the account from the agent's office. Usually these agents are paid by way of an annual management fee from the company, a practice that has been accelerated by the reduction in airline commissions. The benefit to a hotel is that the agent works with the net rates that you have given to the company and does not expect a commission from the hotel.

If you have not given any such special net rates to national companies you can still obtain ad hoc business from companies if you give special rates to the agents. These 'corporate' rates need to be discounted by at least 10 per cent from your regular rates and are commissionable to the agent.

The drawback with business through these in-plants is that you are not able to establish a relationship with the decision maker, since the agent wants to keep you out of the loop, in order to justify their role.

If you are in a location that benefits from international business travel then you will need a way of reaching this potential. Travel agents worldwide use one of the four main GDS (Global Distribution System) to access information about hotels and you will need to ensure that you are featured on all of them.

Through hotel booking and venue finding agents
These specialist agencies have grown up as a result of the reduction of travel personnel within companies who have the time and the inclination to search out the best deals for their company's business travellers. These agents work on behalf of their client companies to find hotel rooms and conference space that suits their brief.

Apart from a few of the larger agencies that work on fees, these booking agents usually charge commission to the hotels so that their service is free to the organisation. For meetings, commission generally needs to be paid on both food and beverage and rooms. You will have to set your own rates but try and avoid increasing commission to 'buy' the business, since in the long run all this does is increase the revenue to the agents and all hotels lose revenue.

These agents will often ask for quotes from a number of hotels and very often reservations get cancelled. Your offer will be one of a number presented to the client, so the better the agent knows your hotel the more likely they are to recommend you. Always respond immediately (within two hours preferably) to any enquiry and do explain when the final offer will be sent. Treat the agent as you would any other prospect but work hard to get the companies to approach you direct in the first place. Always respect the fact that the prospective client is the client of the agent but in the final analysis it is up to the client how they want to book.

◆ TIP ◆

It makes good business sense to make good relationships with some of the reservation staff in the various agencies.

From consortia

There is trend for companies to get together to maximise the use of their buying power. It doesn't happen very much because it has proved quite difficult to get their administration right for both the companies and the hotels. Again the drawback is that you are removed from the decision maker and cannot gauge accurately the benefit to your hotel. Be very wary of giving special rates unless they are more specific about the real travel potential.

Government

The bulk of government business is very price sensitive. Room rates and food allowances are usually set annually and no one has any room for manoeuvre. You can either take the business or not. If you operate in the appropriate price bracket the business can be very regular. Much of it comes through hotel booking or venue finding agencies, so there is the commission issue to account for. Investigate any local prisons or government establishments and treat them like a local company in terms of sales approach.

Local government does generate some demand. They entertain dignitaries from other cities or trade delegations from abroad. There may also be a visit from the appointed twin town. You need to keep in touch with the local contact in the council chambers.

Groups

One off

Groups come in all shapes and sizes and for any number of purposes. It could be a group of 15 on a cultural trip, 45 going to a concert or 50 senior citizens on a Bowls tour. The secretary of the group may contact you direct but more likely you will be approached by a travel agent who will ask you for a quote. If you want the business, then find out exactly the needs of the group (early, late or special meals/room needs etc) and make sure that you include these special arrangements, plus any other ideas you have, in your offer. Be careful of the special needs of senior citizens, particularly related to walking distances, stairs, luggage movement and noise from other guest activities.

If you are in a tourist area, an international conference centre or an incentive destination then there may well be potential from ground handlers.

Ground handlers provide all the local help that an overseas operator needs to make their group's itinerary go smoothly. A ground handler books the coaches, arranges the airport transfers, makes meal reservations and orders tickets for attractions. They also often book hotels, although this is rarely without the involvement of the overseas client, who is the ultimate decision maker.

Series

When a tour operator offers you a series of groups throughout the year it is easy to get carried away. The dates will probably fall across a few of your prime dates, but the rest will be in your off-peak troughs that are difficult to fill. If you accept this series it is quite likely that the peak dates will perform well but as soon as you move into the shoulder period the groups are smaller or are cancelled. You will then have given away some peak days in return for nothing.

Always check the agent's performance, although one year is no guide to what will happen the next. Only accept group series if its non-performance will not have a huge impact on your business; maybe stick to less than 20 per cent of your occupancy?

Health services

A hospital itself is bit like a hotel anyway and indeed there are some very successful hotels actually attached to hospitals.

Convalescing in a hotel is a lot cheaper than tying up a hospital bed. Any hospital is likely to generate a need for hotel rooms, whether these are from patients, relatives, visitors or staff. Make contact initially with the office of the chief executive.

Leisure travellers

Senior citizens

I have included senior citizens here because they are one of the few segments of the leisure market that can travel outside the weekend. Of course you will need to look at the achievable rates since it could be that your weekday corporate business will have a better average rate. Even if this segment is not normally that attractive to you, you need to have some mechanism in place to promote those weeks when business travel reduces, especially around Christmas and other holiday periods. There are specialist websites and magazines that appeal to seniors, so as long as you construct some appropriate offers that are tailored to this market it is possible to generate good business.

It is a mistake to lump all the over 50s together. Although there are now 15 million people over 50 in the UK, they do not conform to the previous stereotype, and each segment needs a different approach.

Weekend visitors

We all know that weekends are three days: Friday, Saturday and Sunday. In some places we can also include Thursdays but that is another problem altogether! There is always the difficult balance of filling all days or at least the Friday *and* the Saturday. Weekend guests are some of the most demanding and time consuming to serve and although their yield might be lower than the weekdays, if you are a corporate hotel the revenue can be the difference between profit and loss.

Whatever your location, there is always something that you can do to promote your weekends. The skill is in promoting something that is appropriate. If you have a city centre location there is no point in promoting a relaxing get-away weekend. It may be true but it isn't what guests expect from a city break. They want to be active and see and do all the activities that are available. If your location is less than perfect then include free transfers to where the action is. The key to success in the weekend market is accurate targeting. You need to package together all those things that are going to excite your target market. Differentiate yourself from the hundreds of options available, be creative and you are halfway there.

Internet

If you include all the local area activity options on your internet site, you give yourself more chances of being found by a search request through a search engine. Speak to all the local suppliers such as airports (flying lessons), race tracks (speed experiences) and ask them if you can put some reciprocal links in your site and theirs; not only will you have some fabulous packages but you will increase your chance of being found from an organic search.

Families/couples

Families can be a good market but depending on the size of your hotel it may be sensible to choose to service families or couples and not both. Business hotel facilities are equally good for weekend guests but couples do seem to have a preference for full size baths: jacuzzis are a bonus but worth a supplement.

Past guests

Your past guests can be a very useful source of fill-up business in less popular times of the year. Make sure that you keep names and addresses and preferably e-mail addresses. For example, if you expect that January and February will be slow you can mail your past guest and offer them a 'past guest special' of, for example, complimentary accommodation as long as they pay for meals. You may not want to promote such a deal publicly but to a discreet list you have a built-in justification.

There are some quite sophisticated ways to keep your list accurate by cross checking against people that have died or have moved. Sometimes the cost of this software and the effort is greater than just sending a letter and seeing if it comes back, particularly if you confine your mailing to those that have stayed within say the last two years only.

Military

If you are near to a military base there could be some demand, although these bases tend to be self-sufficient. Demand is more likely if you are near a naval city, where ships dock and relatives visit to welcome ships back to port.

Depending on the country there is often a distinct armed service travelling segment where special rates do generate overnight stays.

Schools

School-related business comes in many forms, much of its potential related to food and beverage. Teachers often meet every week for an informal lunch but they do also have larger end-of-year parties. The school secretary is the best person to contact.

Boarding schools are a good prospect since they often have parents visiting from a long way away. They come for the beginning and end of term and for speech days. Pupils also have reunions from time to time. Again the school secretary will have details of advertising opportunities.

Show business

Although there are a lot of prima donnas about, this business can be very important. Depending on the quality of your hotel you could accommodate the main artist, the support acts or the back stage crew. The theatre will your first contact point since they will have their programme fixed up to two years in advance.

The nature of their activities makes these guests appear very demanding, but it is usually the timings that are awkward not the service. Artists have been known to regale guests in the bar until the small hours, which is fun for them but not the barman who was expecting to go home at 1am. Good planning is the key, as is making sure you get paid before the impresario leaves the country.

You may well be approached by artist's representatives who will try to convince you that it is in your interest to give them complimentary accommodation for the privilege of having their client to stay. I have never found this to be a very good foundation for a satisfactory relationship. If it fits in with your client profile and you can definitely generate some useful publicity it may be worth considering, but do get a written agreement as to what you are giving and what you are getting.

Sport

Teams

This is a very specialist market and generally more suitable for large hotels with a range of facilities. Teams need extra rooms for staff, a leisure club and very flexible catering. Bookings are made by the team manager or if it is an overseas tour maybe a specialist travel agent. There are also minor and amateur sports that need accommodating but the lack of funds usually means that they choose student or very low cost accommodation.

Teams, particularly football, do look for training facilities in the close season. These teams need easy access to training fields.

Supporters

If you are near to any sort of sports venue there is potential. Even if the sport is minor or amateur and the team doesn't stay in a hotel, there is still potential from supporters and officials. An agent often makes the reservations, but they can also be made by an official from the sport's governing body.

Tourist boards

Local

Local tourist organisations are usually set up to promote a local town or area and are often funded by the local council as well as the tourist attractions. They try not to give any particular priority to any one hotel but that does not mean that you should avoid treating them as a valuable client. If you feel that contributing to their budget is not something that you can refuse, you have to try to get as much business as you can through their office; in season they often get a lot of callers on the day so can be a good source of fill-up business. Give them good rates and don't forget to thank them for their efforts. To make it work for you, consider being appointed to the local tourism committee.

National

Independent hotels are very focused on developing their own business but national tourist activities are aimed at growing the total visitor numbers to the country. You have to decide how much effort and money you are prepared to dedicate to their efforts to grow the size of the cake.

You must be very careful about advertising and events that are set up to promote the whole country. Measuring the outcomes for your hotel individually can be very problematic. For instance even if that journalist from Australia did write something favourable about your hotel in a newspaper in Adelaide, how is it going to really generate extra room nights for you that you can count?

Universities

There is certainly some business from any sort of university, college or further education establishment. Students are a limited market mainly because they don't have much spare money, but they do like to drink and socialise. Many university societies have annual balls and these can be good business. It may be worth taking a stand at freshers' week, where new students go to see what clubs and societies to join. Here is a good opportunity to meet the decision makers on other stands.

Students' relatives are the best potential for bedroom business, particularly at the beginning and end of term and at graduation time. You can advertise in student publications and in the students' union.

For visiting academic staff, accommodation is usually provided at the university but this depends on each college's facilities. Contact the registrar to find out what events they have during the year.

Weddings

Weddings can be a tremendous revenue earner but to make them go well takes a lot of time and dedication. These functions do not suit all hotels, but don't think that because you don't have fantastic gardens or a very large function room it is a market you cannot reach. It may be economic to purchase a marquee, even second hand, and rent it out for the wedding season. Depending when this season finishes it is often worth leaving the marquee erected so that you can promote Christmas parties.

Demand depends on what alternative facilities there are in the local area and you may be surprised at the potential for your hotel. Cost is also a major factor and weddings come in all sorts of shapes and sizes, so there is likely to be a sector of the market that will appeal to you.

Reaching the decision maker is often difficult, which is why you need to make good contacts with the other elements of a wedding arrangement such as dress shops, florists, churches, photographers, printers, limousine hire and so on.

These complementary companies can also form the basis for participants at a bridal fair, preferably in your hotel. You provide the room free and the other participants pay a fee of around £75 to £100 each, which is used for all the advertising and literature that you need. These annual events provide great exposure in the local market and can generate good contacts for later follow up. If you participate in other bridal fairs, stick to your local market. It is unlikely that any fair outside of about ten miles from your hotel will yield much potential.

Much of the wedding market is based on reputation and if you do a good job your business will grow year on year. However you do need to show that you specialise in this market by providing specialist staff and very specific promotional material. There is usually a slight increase in reservations just after Christmas, so be prepared with a plentiful stock of brochures. Remember to take your own photographs of the event; keep these and any special menus and your testimonial letters in a book, which you can show prospective brides (and their mothers).

There is also an increase in demand for civil partnership ceremonies, and you may well find this a profitable speciality.

Many prospects visit hotels at the weekend to check you out by trying your restaurant and visiting your toilets. You need to ensure that there is always someone on duty who can show people around and highlight the main benefits of your hotel. Ensure that you collect at least the following so that the lead can be effectively followed up:

- name and address of both parties;
- telephone number;
- numbers for the wedding breakfast;
- numbers for an evening function;
- timings;
- budget;
- extras list (tick boxes);
- bedroom requirement;
- invoice details.

WHAT CHANNELS CAN YOU USE TO REACH THEM?

You might envy your retail colleagues who make physical products. Often all they have to decide is which retailers to use and whether to use a wholesaler distributor or wholesale direct to retailers. They do not retail from the factory gate and the only way you can get hold of the product is to visit the retailer. All their efforts are directed at 'pulling' demand from the retailer by advertising or sales promotion or 'pushing' demand by retail incentives: a very simple chain.

Contrary to this, in the hotel business we have developed a very complicated set of options involving decisions about selling direct, using a variety of different types of retailer and maybe at the same time wholesaling some room availability. Budget hotels have tried to reduce the options by developing a very effective central reservation organisation based on the internet. Some budget airlines have gone a bit further by only retailing through their website, which is a great solution if you can ensure that your potential customers get to appreciate your total value for money, not just your prices.

So before you try every distribution channel and end up with an administrative nightmare, look through the options and see what suits your circumstances. If you are at the end of a very long delivery chain involving an electronic channel and a travel agent you will obviously pay more costs and commission. On the other hand the rate might be higher, so your net revenue per room may well be better.

Wholesalers often promise good business when you need it but they release unsold rooms back to you at the last minute and they also want net rates that are at least a 30 per cent discount off your full rate, so your net rate will be low. Your decision is about what channel will generate the best net revenue for each particular room each night.

Help with distribution

There are a number of options for independent hotels that want to have help with their distribution strategy. These vary from full franchises where your hotel name is replaced by a brand to simple reservation companies. You do not have to choose any of these, since it is entirely possible to sort out your own strategy. It depends how much you value your independence and how much you want to be in charge of your own destiny.

Brand franchise

The franchising concept is very well developed, particularly for fast food with McDonald's, KFC and Subway. It means that you can operate your business under the umbrella of a name that has already become established with an image in the market place. This only works if you don't have much of a name for yourself and the new brand will bring more guests at a better room rate through an established reservation network. This wider distribution must not be underestimated, since you have to put in a lot of effort to generate leads.

Choice Hotels with its Comfort, Quality, Sleep Inn and Clarion options offers a number of alternatives, as does the Intercontinental Hotels Group that has Intercontinental Hotels, Crowne Plaza, Hotel Indigo, Holiday Inn, Express by Holiday Inn, Staybridge and Candlewood Suites. Different countries have different options for brand franchises and there may well not be any available that suit what you are trying to do. Signing up to a brand franchise is a major business decision, not least because you are then bound to a group of other independent and company-owned properties that might not all be a boost your business. Nevertheless these companies are good at establishing and making sure that you keep to their brand standards. Costs too can be quite considerable, sometimes up to ten per cent of your room revenue. I guess that if you take this option you are no longer an 'independent' hotel!

Consortium/representation

A consortium is a group of independent hotels that join together for the sole purpose of joint distribution and marketing. There is not the same standardisation of approach as a brand franchise but there is some control on the membership, since different consortiums market to different market segments. It is vital that independence is retained, since this is part of the proposition. There are a number of national and international representative organisations but most seem to recruit from the more up-scale sector of the hotel supply. Some organisations recruit on a very obvious concept, such as Relais et Chateau with their dedication to the provision of good food in a classic setting. Others, such as Preferred Hotels, are a little less obvious but have segmented their offer into Summit, Sterling, Boutique and Preferred itself.

Some organisations are more insistent than others on a public show of affiliation. Best Western is such an organisation, which has 4,000 hotel members worldwide. They insist on you putting Best Western on the signage and preceding the name of the hotel wherever it appears within your property. Best Western also has to be mentioned when answering the telephone. This often confuses guests into thinking that it is a conventional hotel group or franchise and you may well lose some business as a consequence.

◆ TIP ◆

In most of these representation companies the 'branding' is very subtle, with little attempt to standardise the product. This lack of standardisation is also a major drawback, since a bad experience with another member can also put guests off your hotel as well.

Each company offers different levels of service for their often-substantial annual fees. However they are a way to reach your market and the range of services can be a great help. These include sales offices, road shows, public relations, exhibitions, training, contracting assistance, leisure programmes, directories, GDS connectivity, meeting sales, web-based reservations and so on.

The advent of the internet has undermined some of the benefits of these consortia since hotels themselves can now do much of this activity. It is also possible just to contract for some of the specific services that you need such as purchasing. Whatever you do depends on your own circumstances, your skills and your needs. Signing up with a representative will not prevent you having to be in charge of your own destiny and drive your business yourself. None provide a guaranteed business 'tap' to turn on and fill your rooms.

Reservation network

Reservation networks are central reservation systems that service multiple hotels in order to gain economies of scale. But this is generally all they do. They do not profess to service only one sector of the market and do not give any guarantee of quality or service standard. They are therefore different to a consortium in that they specialise in reservations not marketing.

Your chain hotel competitors will have their own reservation network, the best known of which is Holidex, serving the needs of Holiday Inn Hotels. Some smaller hotel companies joined together some years ago and set up Supranational, which represents one hotel company in each country in which it operates. UTELL is another general system that takes reservations for most reasonably sized hotels, although they did start out as a representative firm.

These reservation systems also provide an interface with the GDS, enabling you to have direct contact with all the GDS-connected travel agents in the world. This sort of facility is only of benefit to you if you consider that there is potential corporate business through travel agents and you are near a city or an airport. If you are near neither of these the GDS will not be able to locate you.

If you will not benefit from worldwide exposure you can consider a reservation network that only generates enquiries through the internet. In the UK, Active Hotels has developed into a very powerful supplier of business. They provide instant availability and also are an information supplier to a number of other internet sites that promote hotel rooms.

Representative firm

Representative firms can be hired to represent your interests in a particular market that you don't cover yourself. These firms will represent a number of non-competing hotels and will generate leads for you using the variety of tactics that you use yourself. They will have good contacts with meeting planners and producers of corporate business. You will need to pay a fee and also pay for specific marketing actions in addition. Paying by commission rarely works effectively, since there are often disputes as to who actually created the booking.

This type of outsourcing is no longer confined to geographically remote situations. You may well decide to outsource your whole sales process to a third party. I would not recommend this as strategy, since you are leaving your relationship building to a third party, which is not really what the client wants and not what will lead to long-term business growth. You can however outsource some parts of your sales process, such as your daily internet interface, since a specialist contractor can often do this more effectively than you can yourself.

Distribution channel options

You can distribute your rooms direct, through commissionable agents or through wholesalers. Each route has its advantages and disadvantages but your own needs will dictate which distribution channels will work for you. If you can sell all your rooms direct then you will not need to work your way down this list. However every hotel has some times of the year when they need some help, so other options may be attractive.

Direct sales

Selling all your rooms at your published rate direct to your guests is an ideal solution. Not many independent hotels achieve this, although the advent of the internet has given a new lease of life to independent hotels that can now better compete with the chain operators.

◆ TIP ◆

Every room provider should have their own internet site and optimise it to be picked up by searches via the main search engines (Google, MSN and Yahoo!). You can also advertise on these engines in a very cost effective manner through both 'pay per click' and 'pay per impression'.

It is also very effective to make it possible to book rooms immediately off your site. Prospects no longer want to send you an e-mail request and wait for you to answer. This on-line reservation facility can be provided by third parties, some of which also act as intermediaries between your hotel and all the hundreds of internet portal sites that promote hotel rooms. Again there is commission to pay but if you generate a regular guest from these third party internet sites, it is usual for subsequent reservations to come direct via telephone or your own site.

Commissionable retailers

Travel agents and GDS

There are around 180,000 GDS-connected travel agents worldwide who reserve hotels on behalf of business and leisure travellers in return for the payment of commission. Travel agents come in all sorts of shapes and sizes, ranging from the large groups such as American Express and Carlson Wagonlit, often with in-plant offices in large companies, through to individually owned agencies specialising in leisure travel. The critical aspects for all agents is having information on your availability and paying them the commission that is due when they actually make a booking.

In the past the only way for travel agents to get hotel availability and information was from the Global Distribution System (GDS), of which there are four main networks that make up the system: Amadeus (57,000 agents), Galileo (45,000 agents), Sabre (60,000 agents) and Worldspan (20,000 agents). These networks were originally set up for the benefit of their airline sponsors, but very soon the technology was extended to the travel agent offices so that they had real-time information on airline seats.

Very quickly hotel rooms and car hire were added to the offer so that travel agents and airlines could package itineraries for travellers.

Each GDS has a geographical bias based on the home base of the original airline shareholders, but this needn't really concern you unless you want to advertise or pay for priority listing on specific GDS networks and you know where your customers originate. There was a thought that these networks would become redundant as the internet grew, since travel agents could now access your availability from the information you supply to other sources. However it seems that most travel agents use the GDS networks just as much as they ever did.

The GDS networks have also been very quick to take up the new technology and have themselves been at the forefront of the technological advances. For instance Sabre owns Travelocity (and thus LastMinute) and Orbitz used to work closely with Worldspan. However there is likely to be a lot of change in this distribution model that has prevailed since the 1960s. Even the original airlines are not bound to the GDS that they originally set up and each supplier is looking for the lowest cost way to reach the market. The market for distribution products is now deregulated and there are likely to be more entrants who think that they can undercut the incumbents. Hopefully good sense will prevail since what the booker, whether travel agent or travel manager, wants is comprehensive information on all the available options for air travel, hotel rooms and car rental.

So that any agent with a GDS computer can make real-time reservations at your hotel you need a Distribution Service

Provider (DSP) to connect your hotel reservation service to the GDS. There are a number of re-sellers of GDS services as well as organisations such as Pegasus (with its Unires system) which can provide both DSP and reservation services: Wizcom and Trust International are two smaller DSPs.

Travel agents and corporate rate programmes

Some travel agency groups have set up special corporate rate programmes to try to tie corporate travellers to their companies. These can be worth participating in if they are likely to generate a reasonable amount of extra business. Sometimes you have to be in the programme just to be featured by the agent but your representative organisation or reservation company often coordinates participation in these programmes. Consider American Express, Rosenbluth, BTI, Carlson Wagonlit, Woodside and others but bear in mind that participation costs can be heavy.

Commission payments have become more and more vital to travel agents; particularly since fees paid by the traveller have largely replaced airline commissions. It is vital that you set up or participate in a scheme that can remit commission to travel agents as quickly as possible or you will be deleted from the programmes.

Internet companies

The potential for you to reach the leisure traveller have been expanded tremendously by the growth of third party travel aggregators (virtual agents) such as SideStep, Travelocity, Expedia, Orbitz, TripAdvisor, Yahoo Travel and Kayak.

Between them they account for the majority of reservations not made with hotels direct or chain reservation systems. Just like the GDS, they package travel elements together. Participating with these agents can be a problem for small hotels since they work with room allocations and return unsold rooms at 48 hours' notice. The same is true for hotel-only sites such as Hotels.com. Commission rates vary between ten and 20 per cent.

There are also a number of internet sites that specialise in promoting late availability. LateRooms.com, LastMinute.com and Wotif.com all provide a good outlet but the challenge for every hotel operator is not to have rooms that they need to sell through these sites.

Hotel booking and venue finding agents

These agents work on behalf of their corporate or government clients to locate hotel rooms and conference facilities. They offer a free service to their clients and the hotels usually pay them a commission, although you can also negotiate to pay a fee per client. You should treat these agencies in the same way that you would a direct client. Speed of response is paramount, since these agents will usually ask at least three hotels to quote for any specific request. Before you quote find out if the rate is commissionable and at what rate.

These agencies have grown up as a result of the cutbacks made by companies in their dedicated travel departments. So although you might not like these companies inserting themselves between you and the client I suspect that they are a way of life and you will have to live with the situation. Of course if you are active in your prospecting, it will be more likely that you will be in contact with companies before they contact an agent.

Be very careful about being asked for higher levels of commission. It will probably not result in any more business than before and if all hotels agree to it then the only gainer is the agency. However you need to treat each case on its merits. If the standard rate the agency expects is 12.5 per cent there is no point in offering eight per cent since you will not get any business at all.

Incentive houses

Incentive houses specialise in only handling reward travel for their corporate clients. Mostly they only contract with top-of-the-range hotels and usually need meeting space as well as a reasonable number of rooms, often a coach load. They put together an entire trip of which the hotel forms a part. Meals are often organised outside of the hotel. The incentive house relies heavily on the travel providers for their reputation, which puts great pressure on all concerned. Payment is usually net with a management fee from the incentive house but it can be organised on a commission basis.

Wholesalers

Wholesalers, as the name implies, contract to take your rooms usually at a low rate. These rooms will then be sold on to other national or international operators who put together travel packages. The hotel is at the mercy of these operators to make the tours successful, but very often the projected tour will not take place: your rooms will then be returned to you for you to sell yourself through your own channels.

You need to work closely with the operators, since they may need some concessions from you to help them in their marketing efforts. It will not help if you are too strict in your cancellation policy but on the other hand you don't want to be exploited by being promised low season business that doesn't arrive in return for your precious high season availability.

Some wholesalers, such as Superbreak, also have their own product that they retail through the travel trade. This can be useful business but beware of the conditions and the impact on your average rate.

KEY POINTS

- ◆ Articulate your vision anyway you like but ensure that you share it with your customers and your team.

- ◆ There are various levels of support available to help you reach your market. Your circumstances will determine the most appropriate set-up for your hotel.

- ◆ Try to keep your distribution as simple as possible.

- ◆ Be aware of the costs of distribution, particularly in long distribution chains.

- ◆ Wholesalers can be very helpful but be careful about giving away too much without guarantees.

- ◆ Research thoroughly all the opportunities in your area for generating business.

3

What Help Do You Need?

In reality the success of your hotel depends on both the leadership of the owner and the commitment of the staff and particularly the interaction between them. How do you ensure that everyone works together as a team and shares the same vision?

WHAT IS YOUR LEADERSHIP STYLE?

We all understand that whatever goes on in an organisation is influenced greatly by the actions of those at the top. If those in charge are not definite about their own roles and do not organise their own activities efficiently and effectively, then it is unlikely that the rest of the team will be effective either. I have experience of being called to help owners generate extra sales only to find them fully committed in the kitchen. How can you drive a business forward if you are exhausted after 60 hours a week cooking? You have to be organised for success.

> Driving a business forward takes time and application and someone has got to do it. Whatever way you are organised there needs to be a clear definition of who does what and when, and what feedback methods there are for monitoring whether things are going according to plan or not.

I assume that you are committed. I also assume that if there is more than one owner, you are both, or all, committed *and* united. What you need is for every one of your team to be equally committed to the success of your hotel. Unfortunately this is rarely the case.

It is often expected that the business owner or manager alone is responsible for the success of the business. This assumption leads you to take on every task yourself and fail to give responsibility to your staff. Very often the outcome of this for you is a frenetic lifestyle where you never get away from the business. For your employees it is a feeling of disempowerment because they have no clear responsibilities. You then begin to question their commitment and from then on it is a downward spiral with everyone blaming each other and the customer becoming the ultimate loser.

Effective leadership

There is a lot of literature on leadership and it is certainly not my intention to spend too much time on it here. However there are some vital differences between leadership and management that are worth highlighting. Edgar Schein summarises the difference as, 'Leaders create and change cultures, while managers and administrators live within them,' which seems a good enough description. Perhaps it is the difference between being ruled by the heart instead of the head.

The heart involves vision, motivation, support, trust and fun, whereas the head involves issues of goal setting, planning, discipline and procedures. Of course you need both, but you need to recognise when it is appropriate to be a manager and when to be a leader. Or maybe you can separate the roles amongst different people in your hotel?

There is some element of agreement amongst all researchers that the four main characteristics of leaders are:

- A vision of the future.
- The ability to communicate that vision.
- An entrepreneurial spirit.
- A constant quest for excellence by continuous improvement.

I mentioned Richard Branson of Virgin earlier and these characteristics would all seem to apply. He certainly has a vision which he seems very able to communicate and, as he says, 'There is always a market for the best; the bottom line will sort itself out.'

Leaders create a vision of the future and have a desire to change the way things are. They encourage others to come up with new ideas and new ways of approaching their job and are prepared to take risks. Above all, leaders know that they cannot do it all themselves, so they encourage collaboration, build teams and empower others. They always display integrity (consistency between speech and action) since they know their own values and always act in a manner consistent with them. Leaders are always aware of the need to maintain morale, particularly when pursuing the vision is frustrating, so they always celebrate others' achievements and give genuine praise whenever they have the opportunity.

As I said, leadership is different to management, but it can still be learned. There are plenty of organisations that offer helpful training and coaching to help you develop your own leadership skills. We are all born with some gift of leadership and it can be developed if you listen carefully to yourself, understand who you are and stay true to yourself. To be a really effective leader you also need to learn how and when to be a follower. There are circumstances when it is appropriate for you to use others' skills for the long-term realisation of your vision.

If you really do want to develop open communication with your team, never be afraid to admit that you have made a mistake.

This vulnerability will make you appear more human and will encourage others to follow your example.

Key tasks

I can't give you a prescription for a successful organisation. Each hotel is different; you will have certain skills that you have brought to the business and you may or may not have a business background. You may have a partner, business or otherwise, or there may be three of you. All I can do is give you some considerations that you need to take into account as you organise your business for success.

Every hotel, whether it has five rooms or 100, has the same broad operational needs. The only difference is the scale and thus the time needed to carry them out. These key tasks are:

- housekeeping
- maintenance
- accounts/finance
- reservations/reception
- food and drink service
- human resources
- sales.

In a small operation it is likely that you do these all yourself, maybe with a little occasional assistance. You are able to do all the routine tasks in the morning and because you do not cook in the evening, you have time to make the requisite sales calls in the afternoon.

The difficulty starts when you have more than about ten rooms and a busy restaurant. You need to stay open all day, even if there is not much business in the afternoons. Breakfast starts at 7am and you do not finish clearing up in the restaurant until 1am. You try to have one day off a week but you would like two. You still have the seven areas above to manage and that seems to take all day.

A larger and more complex operation will have specialists in many of these areas, particularly food and drink service which breaks down into restaurants, kitchen, bar and meetings. This sort of span of control is difficult to manage, so you will have to make some choices about those issues that you keep day-to-day responsibility for and those that you will hand over to others.

What you will have noticed about the seven core tasks is that six of them involve short-term operational issues and only sales is about the long term. What inevitably happens is that every short-term issue takes priority over your long-term tasks. In principle there is nothing wrong with this: if a waiter fails to turn up, it doesn't help your customers if you don't step in to help because you have an advertisement to write!

Unfortunately this sort of thing happens every day. Even though you have a well structured 'to do' list at the beginning of the week it is still the same at the end of the week. In order to be really effective you need to organise responsibilities within the hotel to allow you to focus your attention on longer-term business development opportunities.

Sales activities

A hotel is like a car; it needs fuel to make it go! And the fuel is a steady stream of customers and guests. If in your case you just open your doors and customers walk into your restaurant and guests call up to make room reservations, all at the right times, and you go on holiday each year and make a good profit, then you are very lucky. Or deluded!

More likely, you make a lot of effort to generate more business. I can't say how much effort you should make or what you need to do, since it depends on your own particular needs. This book sets out the options and some of the tactics that you can employ.

Your actions will be one off, such as:

◆ Competition analysis.

- Brochures and internet site.
- Action plan.

And regular actions such as:

- Past client analysis – why did they stop using you?
- Current clients – develop relationships and mine their hierarchy.
- Prospects – telephone to find more potential.
- Direct mail – develop local potential for restaurant.
- Update website – add new facilities/activities/packages.
- Third parties – update daily with availability and rates.
- Check competition – look at current rates and availability.
- Research – keep eyes open for new housing or corporate moves.
- Agents – send thank you notes and find out if more business is available.
- Local bookers – keep in touch with tourist offices/attractions.
- Joint ventures – look for opportunities to join with complementary services.

This is just the start of the potential. How much time should you allocate to this activity?

Well this depends on how you organise the business development activity. It doesn't have to be done by you. But it is your responsibility to make it happen, so you need to allocate quality time to assessing what has been done and planning what has to be done. In my view, if you are doing all this yourself you should probably allocate 40 per cent of your time to looking after the future. If you have a sales executive that shares the activity then maybe 20 per cent is reasonable.

As I have said before, it is the quality of the time that is vital. Marketing of any sort is about the long-term and you need to have a clear head (and a clear desk!) in order to give it the attention it deserves.

If you find it difficult to get organised, try to allocate a quiet time each day, even if it is just an hour. If, in those five hours per week, you manage to persuade one new client to use you, you will have 50 new clients. Even if each client only gives you ten room nights a year at a rate of £60, then you have generated an extra £30,000 a year. It's all about small steps.

Time management

As I write this, I am aware that I am often frustrated at not planning my time effectively. But I have tried to change and this is the key: it is never too late and whatever your stage of life, there are some real benefits from better planning. There are some great time management strategies published by Time Management International and others too, and I have highlighted some here that you might find useful.

You cannot of course *manage* time; it goes on its merry way without any concerns for anybody. What you can do is *plan* your time so that you can accomplish all your activities and priorities. Three things I have really found useful (and used) are to:

1 List activities

You cannot change what you haven't measured, so for a week or a fortnight keep a diary of exactly what you do each day. Use 15-minute intervals and put down everything, however trivial, including interruptions. This will highlight some areas where you can delegate tasks or maybe make yourself unavailable.

2 Prepare a 'To do' list

This list is only the start, since it will include a whole host of things, only some of which will have a big impact on your business. The next task is to prioritise. Use your personal organiser or just some paper cards but put a priority against every task and do not go to task two unless you have finished task one.

Maintaining focus is the biggest contributor to planning your time effectively. If you have clear goals, you will do everything you can to make sure you accomplish them. You will be less prone to interruptions and will not be distracted.

3 Control paperwork

The greater use of computers has seemed to increase rather than decrease the amount of mail that crosses your desk. All mail, and that includes e-mail, should be handled/read only once, during which time you decide what to do with it:

- ◆ Do something now – if you know what to do, then get on the phone, write a reply or whatever, but do it now.

- ◆ Delegate to someone else – can or should someone else deal with this? Is dealing with this matter a waste of your time?

- ◆ Defer until later – there are occasions when you need more information or you need to think through a solution. Put it on your priority list and allocate time to it.

- Dump it – if you don't need it then file it in that round basket or delete it. You will never miss it. The most vital e-mail discipline is to keep your inbox empty by using the filing system in your management system (e.g. MS Outlook, MS Outlook Express, Lotus Notes or some other software).

Other strategies to manage your time:
- Set regular times each day to deal with e-mail.
- Deal with things straight away if you can – for complaints get straight on the phone.
- Delegate as much as you can.
- Ask yourself 'Why am I doing this?' and then change.
- Time block your day for particular tasks – it helps you focus.
- Turn off your mobile.
- Only spend your time with good prospects.
- Only schedule productive meetings.
- Put holidays and networking events in your diary in advance otherwise you will be 'too busy'.

Work/life balance

If you are really involved in the business, it is often difficult to distinguish between work and your personal life: they almost become one and the same. If you don't make an effort to schedule (goal setting again!) specific actions that retain a good work/life balance you will undermine your effectiveness as a leader.

But it is not just about your own balance. You need to set a good example to your staff about their needs too. I read a recent survey that found that around 70 per cent of managers (and directors) are looking for a greater sense of 'meaning' in their working lives. Working longer hours than contracted and working in an organisation that was not environmentally and socially responsible caused most of this lack of 'meaning'.

◆ TIP ◆

It is particularly important to be aware of the need for balance in your team, since some of them will have caring commitments for children and relatives that can be difficult to rearrange, particularly at short notice.

The hospitality business can be very greedy with your time and working long hours can become a habit. Unlike many project-based businesses where the location of where you do your job is unimportant, giving service to the public does involve you (or somebody) actually being there. This business can also be so addictive that you neglect your domestic arrangements. At work there is always a buzz, which somehow evaporates when you have to mow the lawn at home. But there is no need to worry because you can always be found on the end of a mobile!

There is a lot of truth in the old adage that 'all work and no play makes Jack a dull boy'. The secret is in balance. Work can be hard and it can take up any number of hours you like, but there must be other things in your life to balance out the work.

Physical health
You are no use to anyone unless you are fit. Just do a little exercise each day and make sure that you eat healthily. It is easy to fall into bad eating habits.

Family/relationships

Spend time with your immediate family and your relations. However successful your business, your children will not thank you for not being there as they grow up.

Friends

It's vital that you have some fun.

Recreation/holidays

You will never have a holiday unless you put the dates in your diary.

Your mind

Always keep learning. Go on some courses, read a book or listen to music.

The community

Give some of your time and effort unconditionally to a local charity or worthy cause.

SHOULD YOU EMPLOY A SALES SPECIALIST?

How do you decide whether or not to employ a sales specialist? Again this really depends on your own skills and aptitudes and the potential of your business. There are many sales situations where potential contacts really benefit from speaking direct to the owner or manager. On the other hand there is a lot of research and routine follow up that can be organised by a sales executive. But what you cannot avoid is the need to have a sales focus within your hotel. Without this focus your business will inevitably suffer and you risk disappointing all those 'warm' prospects that phone. If you do not feel comfortable with selling then either get comfortable through training or bring people into your hotel that are comfortable.

Mostly it is a question of economics. If your occupancy of a 30 room hotel is 55 per cent and the rate you expect from extra business to take you to 70 per cent is £50 net, then the potential is £82,150 each year. Say that you have to pay a sales executive £25,000. Is the extra revenue interesting?

Don't forget the 55 per cent that you already have. It takes a lot of effort to keep that sort of occupancy, since just by natural attrition you can lose up to 25 per cent of your business each year: companies move, your contact moves, the competition undercuts your rates, the expense policy changes or any number of other reasons.

What you cannot do is pass on your responsibility for producing top-line revenue. You have to stay involved in the sales activities and probably look after certain sales accounts yourself. You also need to be involved with in-house sales training and in this way provide effective leadership.

Responsibilities

I highlighted earlier some of the sales tasks. In addition there is a great deal of work to be done within the hotel by a sales specialist to make every team member part of the greater 'sales team'. Reception staff need to be helped to up-sell to more expensive rooms and banqueting or meeting specialists need to be motivated to up-sell to better menus.

◆ **TIP** ◆

Reception staff sometimes complain that they are too busy to do anything except check people in but in a small hotel this is pretty weak excuse. Their willingness to sell can be influenced by how you motivate and empower the whole team.

Who does what is up to you to decide, but the training needs internally mustn't be underestimated. Even where you have reception or banqueting managers there needs to be a system for ensuring that the sales training is undertaken.

Recruitment

Although the type of selling that takes place in a hotel is relatively soft, it is nevertheless difficult to stay motivated through the inevitable setbacks that a sales executive receives. You need someone with persistence and the ability to see things through. It is not a job for instant gratification. Look at the applicant's CV for examples of where they have had to use their initiative.

Ideally they will come from a sales background, but don't be fooled by hotel-type job descriptions such as 'banqueting sales'; usually this is nothing of the sort. There is a big difference between actually getting on the phone and waiting for it to ring. I have always favoured people from outside the hospitality industry, usually selling business to business; membership development staff from health clubs seem to have the right attitude.

A good sales executive in a hotel will get involved in management and training so, although they might not have these skills, you need to be convinced that they can develop them.

The sales executive will often be the first impression that prospects have of your hotel. So if he or she does not make a great first impression on *you* then be very wary. You shouldn't have any trouble at the interview because the sales candidate should do most of the talking. Of course you don't want someone who is going to bore your prospects with too much talk and not enough listening but the only really effective tool that a sales person has is their mouth and the words that come out of it. So they need to be quick thinkers, persuasive talkers and good at writing. In my view the most vital attributes are an interest in people and a genuine smile that involves the mouth *and* the eyes.

Managing and motivating

The most effective thing that you can do for a sales executive is make it easy for them to do their job. You need to give them your wholehearted support and ensure that there is no friction between sales and operations. Each separate part of your organisation needs to be educated about all the others. Sales need to understand the technical and operational limitations of what they can offer and operations need to understand how the sales process works and their part in it. Entertaining clients to lunch must not be seen as total pleasure but as part of a very serious effort to sustain everyone's livelihood.

Small amounts of public praise go a long way and your consistent encouragement will often be better than financial incentives. Look for any small sales success and try to avoid criticism. If you do put in a system of financial incentives, they work much better if they are based on activity goals, which will be related to the identified needs of the hotel.

Evaluating

Sales staff tend to be very goal orientated and you need to agree some specific goals with them and evaluate them from time to time. You should never ask that a certain number of calls be done each day but look at useful metrics:

◆ New business starts (if you are trying for new corporate business).

◆ Conversion of enquiries from quotes (if you are sending out group or meeting quotes).

◆ Number of show rounds (if you are trying for new corporate, meeting or wedding business).

◆ Conversion of brochure requests/internet enquiries to actual business (if you are promoting weekend business).

◆ Room up-sells per month (if you have the facility).

You can also look at some softer issues such as cooperation with other departments and fulfilment of sales training tasks.

Meetings

A good sales executive is inclined to action rather than introspection so the fewer meetings the better. However you will probably see the sales executive informally fairly frequently, so you need to schedule some formal time to reflect on what has gone well and what hasn't. I would recommend a weekly meeting (outside of prime contact time) to talk about the forecast for the next few months and decide on some strategic actions if necessary, particularly with regard to the internet and pricing. You can also discuss the good and bad aspects of last week's sales actions, talk through the specific plan for the week ahead and agree what assistance is needed from you to help the sales process with specific prospects.

Attributes of a successful sales person

You will know that you have a good sales executive if you can identify most of these attributes in your specialist:

+ **Daily disciplines.** They will break down their goals into daily activities based on their knowledge of how many calls they need to make to achieve a user.

+ **Ability to prioritise.** They will concentrate on those prospects likely to produce new revenue rather than make easier calls to already loyal customers. They will cancel a networking lunch if a good prospect offers them a meeting.

+ **Understanding revenue.** They will know that the name of the game is revenue not rooms and will be aware of the implications of room rates and RevPAR (revenue per available room) but will also think about total spend in pursuing different business possibilities.

+ **Remains optimistic.** They learn from their setbacks and develop tactics to offset them. They remain focused and demonstrate that they really care.

+ **Initiative.** They will feel ownership of your hotel's sales performance, will display initiative to solve clients' issues and will be creative.

+ **Urgency.** They are never complacent and stay focused on keeping on top of their plan.

Alternatives

An alternative to a specialist sales executive is to look at the skills and ambitions of your team and see if there is any useful downtime that could be utilised within the shifts. This is not entirely satisfactory since sales development is a long-term task and most operational issues are immediate. The immediate always has priority so any agreed sales development activity always takes second place. However something is always better than nothing, although you need to ensure that every contact with a prospect reflects your image and culture.

HOW CAN YOU CREATE A COMMITTED TEAM?

It is obvious, but nevertheless true, that the activities of the people you employ will determine the quality of service you deliver to your customers. Having happy and motivated staff with the right skills will make for happy guests. It is also a truism that you should recruit your team members for their attitude since, by and large, everything else can be learned.

It doesn't matter what function the person fulfils within your organisation, there are some common characteristics that are very important. Some of these characteristics may seem difficult to identify but they illustrate what you should be looking for when recruiting a new employee. Finding someone with them all may be like searching for the Holy Grail and you may have to develop some of them by coaching and training later on.

What makes a good employee

A good employee should:

- be professionally competent;
- be loyal to their colleagues and the goals of the business;
- be flexible and willing to change;
- be helpful and co-operative across the organisation;
- be cost-conscious and not waste resources;
- feel responsible for both success and failure of the business;
- use their initiative for the benefit of the business;
- work conscientiously to maintain and develop quality;
- treat their colleagues with respect and dignity;
- learn from their mistakes;
- be open and honest;
- be self-reliant;
- have self-discipline and stamina.

But perhaps the most important characteristics which you need your employees to display are:

- responsibility
- loyalty
- initiative.

Responsibility

It is easy to despair of ever having a committed team. Owners become very sceptical of their employees ever displaying the sort of commitment that they display themselves. You can reduce this commitment gap by having your employees feel responsible for the results of your hotel.

Responsibility, however, is a two-way street. Not only must you give responsibility and authority to your staff but also they must be willing to take responsibility. Giving responsibility is one of the most powerful ways of taking advantage of the natural energy, talents and creativity of your employees. Taking responsibility is one of the best ways to develop personally and create a meaningful life.

◆ TIP ◆

The main reason that efforts to give staff more responsibility do not have the expected results is that managers do not give enough power and freedom of action along with the responsibilities.

People feel responsible when they:

- ◆ have something to be responsible for;
- ◆ are aware of the goals;
- ◆ feel that they have influence.

The experience of being able to influence a situation makes people feel important and creates hope and expectation of progress. It strengthens their self-esteem, which enables them to take more responsibility. Once staff members have accepted some element of responsibility they automatically start to take on wider issues. They will consider their own development, the development of their department or area and the development of the hotel.

To get the most out of life everyone needs to take responsibility for their own actions. Each person chooses the life they live. You will recognise staff that feel they are victims of circumstances by the excuses they give. For example, an employee might say, 'I'm sorry I'm late but my car wouldn't start.' What they should say is, 'I am sorry I am late but I failed to ensure that my car was in good working order.'

Here is an ideal opportunity to talk to your team member about taking ownership of their problems and solving them themselves.

Loyalty

When employees feel responsible for your hotel's performance, then they are in a position to be loyal. They will then be proud of your hotel, defend it when necessary and make constructive suggestions for improvement.

Loyalty, however, is an opportunity for conflict. Although you want all your team to be loyal to the business, people sometimes have conflicts with their family commitments. Conflicts also arise when all members of the team do not pull their weight, or a team member notices a colleague making repeated mistakes which managers ignore.

Staff who are not loyal are very disruptive in any organisation. Anyone making negative remarks about the hotel or their colleagues, or not taking responsibility for failures (blaming other people), should be encouraged to seek alternative employment. The loyal employees will expect this to happen and are likely to feel disgruntled when it doesn't.

Loyalty is about doing everything for the long-term benefit of the hotel. This does not mean saying 'yes' to every request. It should mean that if a team member does say 'yes' they will do everything they can to achieve the task. It also means that anyone should be allowed, and expected, to say 'no', if they cannot perform the task to the required standard.

Initiative

Staff who feel responsible for the success of the hotel, and are loyal, are likely to be prepared to display their initiative. This can be in minor areas such as dealing with guests' complaints or making major suggestions to innovate your service delivery.

To encourage staff to display their initiative you need to give them the freedom and the opportunity. It is also vital that the goals of the hotel are fully understood and accepted so that everyone is pulling in the same direction.

Employing family members

When you operate a hotel just with family members there is generally no real problem. Well, apart from the usual issues that arise in families about everyone doing their fair share etc! Even in this situation it is wise to be clear about job descriptions and responsibilities, particularly where young people or more distant relatives are involved.

The real problems arise when you employ family members in addition to other people. Blood is always thicker than water, which makes it very difficult to evaluate fairly the contribution of your relatives. All the normal relationships between employees go out of the window since the family member, however hard they try to fit in, is always seen as having a direct line to the boss. All the various feedback mechanisms fail, with none of the family getting the real picture about the business or their own performance.

I remember working for a fairly large private hotel company in the South Pacific when the owner sent his *optician* son-in-law to work in corporate head office. It seemed amusing at the time imagining where his particular skills were being applied but it caused a lot of dissatisfaction, particularly about his salary. I am sure it all seemed very straightforward from the owner's point of view since it was his business. However, it caused a lot of resentment and confusion.

There are many examples of entrepreneurs in the hotel business trying to 'keep it in the family', and few of them have been successful. However good your son might be in the business, there is always that nagging doubt about whether he would, or could, have succeeded on his own. I recall a colleague of mine mentioning a conversation he had had with his boss who happened to be the son of the owner of the business. The son admitted that his father couldn't really sack him because he would still have to support him!

A group of employees or a team?

We often call our group of employees a team, but do we really organise things so that they are able to work like one? Are you convinced that all the good qualities displayed by your local sports team are displayed by your employees? Can you answer 'yes' to the questions below?

◆ Do you work together towards a common goal?
◆ Is everyone committed?
◆ Does everyone do their best at all times?
◆ Do you have fun?
◆ Are you proud to be in the team?
◆ Does everyone feel responsible for the successes and failures of the team?
◆ Does everyone work for themselves *and* the team to succeed?

If you answered 'no' to some of them, then you need to take some positive action to develop team working. For everyone to do their best you must specify exactly what is expected from them. They should all contribute to the success of the business but it is vital that they understand exactly how success is measured.

Characteristics of a successful team

If your team is to be successful and achieve the results you expect, they must have:

◆ the right tools for the job;
◆ a positive attitude;
◆ the necessary competence (skills and motivation);
◆ fairly allocated responsibilities and tasks.

The characteristics of a successful team are that:

♦ Goals and tasks of the team are both understood and accepted by each individual.
♦ Responsibilities and roles are clearly allocated.
♦ Everyone feels free to express their feelings and opinions.
♦ People support and encourage each other.
♦ Disagreements are not suppressed or overridden.
♦ Individuality is encouraged to achieve team goals.
♦ Criticism is frequent, frank and relatively comfortable.
♦ Performance standards and rules are clear.
♦ When action is taken, clear assignments are made and accepted.
♦ Goals of the individual and the team are aligned.

Organisational conflicts

There are three key factors involved in the success of any organisation. You will want to achieve the best in all three but they are so interlinked that conflicts can arise:

1 Productivity

Productivity is the optimum use of all resources (including human resources) to create results. Companies need to be productive to survive. Individuals need to be productive in order to function well in their job, retain self-esteem and contribute to the team effort.

In order to create positive results it is vital to:

♦ define the goals;
♦ define the tasks to reach the goals;

- determine when and by whom the tasks should be done;
- apply resources, time and energy to these tasks.

2 Relationships

Relationships both within the organisation and with the outside world are about company culture, communication and how people are treated. The business is likely to be more successful if employees enjoy their work, have a good work/life balance and really believe that they work for a caring organisation. People who feel good about themselves and others are likely to be motivated to do their best under the most difficult circumstances.

3 Quality

Customers have an expectation of quality, which you may or may not consider reasonable. It is vital to define the quality you expect and then measure how close you are to achieving it. The goal is to close the gap with the help of your team.

Links between productivity, relationships and quality

You need to keep looking for new ways to increase your productivity, improve relationships and develop quality. But these areas are so interlinked that actions in one area can cause a negative change elsewhere:

- You cannot expect receptionists to deliver high quality service (*quality*) to guests if communication between departments is poor and they don't feel valued (*relationships*).

- Attempts to cut costs (*productivity*) may lead to lower standards of service (*quality*) and therefore have an impact on how customers feel (*relationships*).

Sharing the workload

As I mentioned before, the typical owner of a hotel has an extremely wide range of responsibilities. You cannot possibly perform all the tasks yourself so you have to divide them up somehow. You have to delegate responsibility. This is a major commitment on your part, in terms of both time and effort. Sometimes it is tempting to say to yourself, 'It's quicker to do it myself rather than spend time explaining it to someone else.' This may be true in the short term but it does not solve the long-term task problem and it definitely disempowers your team member (more about this later on).

Delegation does not relieve you of ultimate responsibility. What it does is give authority to a staff member to carry out the designated tasks using whatever tools are necessary and to an agreed timescale. Hopefully they will feel that they can use their initiative to achieve what has been agreed.

On a day-to-day basis you do not need to make all the decisions. How often are you asked what you consider to be a stupid question? It is far better to push the decision-making down the organisation to its most appropriate level.

Some major advantages of delegation are:

♦ decisions are made at the right level;
♦ your time is released to do more productive tasks;
♦ staff skills are used appropriately and developed;
♦ operations continue when the owner is absent;
♦ the workload is more fairly distributed.

However, to make delegation work you must trust, recognise, and make rules.

Trust

You need to work on the assumption that everyone will respond positively to the opportunity to take responsibility. You will never know how they can perform unless you give them the chance. You cannot be half-hearted about it. Believe in your team and most of the time they will live up to, and probably exceed, your expectations. You might also learn different ways of doing things.

> If staff make mistakes, as they inevitably will, give them another chance and treat it as a learning experience. Everyone knows when they screw up, so you don't need to add to their grief!

Recognise

Recognition is vital to effective delegation. Not only recognise when staff have performed a task but also look for other opportunities, such as if they do something really helpful. Don't forget to pass on recognition you get personally for tasks that were actually carried out by members of your team.

Make rules

For delegation to work staff need to know:

- ◆ What is to be done.
- ◆ How much authority they have.
- ◆ Why the task is to be done.

- How the task should be done.
- When the task should be completed.
- What the priority is.
- Likely problems.
- Feedback required.

Coaching for better delegation

Obviously you can't just say to a team member, 'Here is a new task, it's now yours, go away and get on with it.' You need to prepare the ground and ensure that the team member is in a good position to accept the new tasks that you would like them to take on. You must try to find out why anyone is reluctant to take on a new work task. To be an effective delegator you need to be aware of how your coaching skills can smooth the path for the person to whom you are delegating. This delegated work should always represent an opportunity for genuine advancement in terms of skill and responsibility.

Coaching is the art of improving the performance of others. It attempts to close the gaps between an individual's present level of performance and the desired one. It is a continuous process of setting goals and then helping get them achieved. One useful model to use in goal setting is the **GROW** model:

- Define the performance Goals.
- Understand the Reality of what is going on at the moment.
- Explore the Options for achieving the goals.
- Agree When the tasks will be done.
- Implement the agreed actions.
- Feedback on how things went.

This process should take place whenever you interact on a formal basis with your team. You will also need to decide the most appropriate way to coach different team members. Initially some will need to be directed more than others, but the long-term aim should be to let employees do most of the talking so that they set their own goals and find their own solutions. They are likely to be more committed than others who may have been more closely directed by you.

The hospitality industry has always championed practical skills rather than academic learning. To be a top performer you need to be able to influence others and be sensitive to their feelings, whether these are your colleagues or your guests. These issues of 'emotional intelligence' rather than 'academic intelligence' were highlighted by Daniel Goleman in his 1996 book *Emotional Intelligence – why it can matter more than IQ*. He contends that people with emotional intelligence are:

- **Self-aware**: People who are self-aware know how they feel and how they are likely to react in any given situation.

- **Self-regulated**: People who are self-regulated are able to accept and manage their own feelings. They work well within teams and develop good working relationships. They remain in control when conflicts arise and encourage staff to do the same. They recognise their own limitations and their need for a sensible work/life balance.

- **Motivated**: People who are motivated have the desire to excel for themselves and the hotel. The skill is to link their desire to succeed to improving your hotel's service.

You can help yourself and your team to improve everyone's emotional intelligence by collectively reflecting on your experiences and learning from them. You need to be willing and able to give and receive feedback that helps you all see yourselves through other people's eyes. Your team members can then be encouraged to take responsibility for their own results and pursue challenging goals. This requires quite a high level of self-confidence and skill on the part of a manager but is really the key to progressing from delegation to empowerment.

What is empowerment?

As I said earlier, delegating responsibility implies that this responsibility can be taken back and is often seen as a temporary arrangement for the benefit of the giver not the taker. The hotel organisation continues to be a typical pyramid structure (hopefully kept as flat as possible) with some tasks pushed down the organisation to be done by the most appropriate person.

Empowerment, however, is not about temporary *delegation* but about *devolution*, which is a permanent change. The manager is no longer at the top of the pyramid in a traditional controlling position supported by his or her staff. In the empowered organisation the manager plays a supporting role at the bottom of an inverted pyramid by facilitating, consulting, coaching and mentoring staff so that they are enabled to reach the organisation's service goals. Leading is from behind not from the front.

◆ TIP ◆

Empowerment is a productive way to get the best from yourself and your staff. It places real power where it can be used most effectively, close to the customer. It means that tasks are devolved together with responsibility and decision-making.

There are several books on the subject available if you wish to read further. My intention here is just to highlight some of the benefits should you really be committed to enhancing the whole culture of your service by empowering people in your organisation.

There have been significant changes in the education of young people over the last few years. The advent of computers and the internet has revolutionised the availability of information. Some of us remember learning tables by rote and remembering facts by the bucket-load. There is no longer any need for this. What is important now is knowing where to find information. This has bred a more initiative-led culture where young people are encouraged to take responsibility for their own learning.

Many hotels have traditional cultures with people 'in authority' directing staff to carry out tasks in a predetermined way. There is then a culture clash between young people having to work in a parent/child situation that they thought they had left behind. Unfortunately some staff and some managers actually like this parent/child relationship. It enables the manager to feel that they are 'in charge', and can dispense tasks and rewards and make rules to ensure compliance. Staff like it because they can act out whatever role suits them (e.g. sulky teenager, naughty rebel, princess etc) and be rewarded if they are 'good'.

These relationships do not benefit anyone and are certainly not the way that adults should relate to each other. Staff need to be helped to grow so that work relationships become truly adult/adult.

Profile of an empowered organisation

There are a number of aspects of an empowered organisation that contribute to effective implementation. Most are about your attitude to staff and the way that you deal with them on a professional basis.

Trust

This is the most important factor in the success of an empowered organisation. It is demonstrated mostly by your willingness to tolerate mistakes that are made in pursuit of your goals. Staff need to feel that you trust them to take risks and will tolerate the errors that might occur. You need to be able to praise the reasons for taking the actions, even if an error was the outcome. This is not to say that you have to put up with incompetence or the repetition of avoidable errors.

Staff need to feel that they can admit to making a mistake. They need to believe that they are more likely to be criticised for not trying, rather than for not succeeding. The last thing you want is for mistakes to be covered up as so often happens, since this does not help you improve your service.

Openness

In a climate of openness staff will feel able to voice their concerns and criticism in the same way that they admit their mistakes. They should feel able to let you know whether or not you are providing the right guidance and support that they need to perform their tasks.

To be completely open you also need to keep them fully informed about your plans and even your thoughts. You need to share with your staff so that they share with you.

Goals

An empowered organisation is underpinned by a set of shared goals by which everyone judges their success. If everyone knows where you are going it is more likely that you will get there. Everyone needs to buy in to what you are striving for, so they need to be part of the process. It just will not work if you pin up a mission statement in the locker room! You need to create a shared vision about the kind of organisation you want to be.

Appraisal and training

Traditional appraisal systems can often be a very one-sided affair with comments flowing from manager to staff. More effective is a system where individuals feel responsible for assessing their own performance and progress. Personal objectives and individual tasks are aligned with business objectives and are set by open negotiation between manager and staff. Appraisals also give staff an opportunity to comment on how their manager is performing.

Of course, since staff have objectives, they also need the tools to help them achieve them. During an appraisal it is important to analyse the skill and knowledge gaps that staff believe they have and make plans to fill them. Training is an essential commitment from the company and needs to be budgeted for, and thought of as an investment rather than an expense. This does not mean that there is a free-for-all in going on expensive external courses. Often the skill gaps can be filled by on-the-job training from peers or supervisors or by coaching from managers.

Communication

In most hotels, where information flows at all, it is usually downwards. This is not really communication at all, which is essentially a two-way process. Difficult as it may be, it is vital to open a channel that allows staff to contribute by asking and telling. This is another aspect of openness, since it is important for the development of customer service excellence that staff feel free to share errors and problems for the mutual benefit of the organisation.

Benefits of empowerment

There are many benefits for you, the organisation and your customers. It allows hotels to respond quickly and flexibly to customer and market demands, and staff to become fully utilised.

Customer service

As customers, we have all come up against the staff member who does not have the authority to sort out our problem or does not seem to care that their actions prevent us from ever using the company again. They have their job and they are going to stick to the rules otherwise they will get into trouble.

I recall visiting an outlet of a well-known restaurant chain that had run out of rice and yet there was a shop only five minutes away. What possible objective could the manager have been set that prevented her buying some rice?

Is your organisation like this? Does your waiting team really care enough to pass back comments to the kitchen? Do the chefs accept it all with good grace and use the feedback constructively?

In an empowered organisation staff manage their relationships with customers as they see fit, using their initiative and understanding of customer expectations.

> Do your staff know that the overriding task is to ensure that customers are so delighted that they will return? What latitude have you given them to achieve this? What is their authority to resolve customer complaints?

If someone does make a complaint you need to find out how best to compensate them. What is going to make them feel that they have come out of the situation with their self-esteem intact? A particularly effective approach is to ask this question, 'I am sorry that our service is not up to your expectations, but I want to make sure that you are satisfied. Given the circumstances, what would you like me to do that would be fair?'

The word 'fair' is very powerful and should prevent you from being asked for anything outrageous but, even if you are, at least you have set up a dialogue that should lead to a mutually satisfactory outcome.

Motivation

Staff who have the opportunity to enhance their skills have a greater sense of achievement. The job they do is seen as being more important, and they feel that they can make a real impact on the organisation.

Less stress

Research shows that stress is often caused by lack of control over your work activities. Workers on a factory line suffer more stress than managers who can organise their own daily activities. Empowerment increases staff's sense of control by enabling them to make more of their own decisions about what they do and how they do it.

Organisational effectiveness

In a rapidly changing world where there is a need to react quickly, you need staff who can respond without having to seek advice or permission all the time. Managers need to place more trust in their staff's skill and knowledge. Empowerment helps to remove the blocks on performance that traditional management approaches can produce.

Management skills

An empowered organisation is one that does not allow poor managers to evade their responsibilities. Indeed, managers probably need to be more skilled than before. These skills are however more difficult to acquire since they are people skills. Management becomes more collaborative, with application of more encouragement than direction. Relationships become more adult/adult and managers achieve results by being *an* authority rather than being *in* authority.

Traditional management skills include, amongst others:

- planning
- communicating
- co-ordinating
- motivating
- controlling
- directing
- leading.

In an empowered organisation there will be less emphasis on the last three. In addition a manager will now need the additional skills of:

- enabling
- facilitating
- consulting
- collaborating
- mentoring
- supporting.

Leadership is now from behind, rather than from the front. Managers will recognise the skills and knowledge of the front-line staff and will harness these to achieve the agreed organisational goals.

Time

In a traditional organisation the owner or manager retains a lot of day-to-day responsibility and feels the need to check that everything is being done as it should be. Where empowerment is fully in place, responsibility is devolved to the team, maybe with managers in the background looking after strategy. This leaves you more free time to dedicate to securing the future of your business, knowing that the day-to-day interactions between your customers and staff are in capable, responsible hands.

WHAT INCENTIVES CAN YOU USE?

Finding good incentive schemes that deliver both improved results for the hotel and the right benefits for the staff is no easy task. You might consider that it is everyone's job to sell and provide excellent service, so why should employees have an extra reward just for doing their job? You may already have tried a number of ideas that failed to produce the expected results.

Unintended consequences

The downfall of many schemes is often the 'unintended consequences'. For instance, you can give reception staff an incentive with a bonus for each upgraded room they sell on check-in. They then become so focused on this that if a guest merely asks for road directions they are treated in an off-hand manner and feel that the service is poor. The same applies in a restaurant where efforts to drive wine sales are directed at customers irrespective of whether or not they are a prospective wine drinker; customers can then feel pressured and resentful.

Non-financial incentives

Your own circumstances will dictate what sort of schemes might work. If you only have a few staff then something very personal keeps up motivation, such as away-days, after-shift get togethers, and up-selling prizes. I know of a few hotels that reward extra effort with their own internal 'money' that staff can spend in their own unit or in other hotels in the group.

Financial incentives

If you have a larger operation with a manager in charge, then it can provide effective leadership if a good proportion (up to 25 per cent?) of his or her salary package is assessed on delivering an operational profit, based on those aspects that they can control.

However it is important for the management team to have both long-term and short-term incentives. The long-term scheme could focus on commitment to the organisation over three to five years, with whatever they have earned from the scheme being converted at some stage into cash or shares.

For any formal scheme to work, staff must first of all feel part of an empowered organisation. You can then work out with each staff member those key aspects of their job that will deliver above-average results for the hotel. For instance, for a receptionist their Key Performance Indicators (KPI) can be the number of guests taking dinner in-house, the number of executive rooms sold and the average room rate each day. An incentive scheme can then be introduced that rewards success in any of these areas; say £1 for each diner booked in to the restaurant and £5 for each up-sell to an executive room. Similar schemes can be introduced for all staff, from room cleaners (control of room consumable costs) to accounts (reduction in creditors).

Of course you need to balance the enthusiasm that staff develop in their own areas with the impact these can have on your guests. For example, any incentive for the chef to reduce food costs must not involve any reduction in quality standards, but then this is just another management issue.

Devising a scheme

However, developing a successful scheme needs considerable care and involving the team might enable you to devise a scheme that suits everyone. No one wants their pay to be totally reliant on team performance, not least because teams are often fluid and sometimes don't last for very long without personnel changes. A good basis may be to keep individual incentives, which satisfy basic human needs, and then in addition have everyone receive the same percentage of salary in addition as a team bonus.

One important feature is that people want more from their jobs than their pay. They want recognition for extra effort or valuable contributions to the business. If you are going to reward someone make sure that they are seen to be receiving it. Presentation and delivery can be just as memorable as the reward itself.

If staff feel involved and committed in the first place, they are likely to respond favourably to any scheme that you introduce as long as they consider it fair. The essential elements of any incentive scheme are to:

- Keep it simple.
- Reward individual *and* team performance.
- Make it fun and interesting.

- Pay cash earned on time.
- Continually communicate progress.
- Not have money the only focus: non-cash rewards can work just as well.

KEY POINTS

- Provide effective leadership and make working with you fun.

- Define who does what in your organisation and set everyone, including yourself, some realistic goals.

- If you employ sales specialists, work *with* them to achieve your revenue objectives.

- Communicate with your team by talking to them, but also listen and act.

- Continually develop the skills of your team.

- Understand the aspirations of your people and help them achieve them.

- Empower your team so that they deliver superior customer service.

- A well thought-out incentive scheme usually produces benefits for your hotel and for the team.

Part Two
Reaching Your Prospects

Chapter 4 Using Personal Contact
Telephone
Direct contact
Networking

Chapter 5 Direct Marketing
Direct mail
E-mail
Newsletters

Chapter 6 Advertising

Chapter 7 Media Relations

Chapter 8 Promotional Materials and Activity
Sales promotion
Brochures
Your internet site

'Talk less; you will automatically learn more, hear more, see more and make fewer blunders.'

Mark McCormack

4

Using Personal Contact

If you know who your prospects are then personal contact is the most effective way to reach them. You can tailor an individual approach and gain vital feedback if you listen well. You can build a relationship with an individual, understand their needs and feed this information back to the business in order to make improvements.

TELEPHONE

The telephone is a very powerful tool. If it were not, then why does nearly everyone have a mobile? Unfortunately the telephone isn't used enough in the hotel business. Is this because you are scared of it? There is no need. So long as you are clear about your objectives it can become a very valuable friend.

Incoming calls

Every time the phone rings you should cheer; it is the result of all your efforts (unless it is someone selling you something or chasing a payment!). You must not waste the opportunity that has been presented to you. It can be very helpful to have strict procedures for anyone handling these incoming calls, even if you answer them all yourself.

Know your costs

It is very useful to measure just how much it has cost you to get that call. Add up all your advertising, mailing and sales costs (e.g. £1,200 per month) and divide by the number of calls received (250). Each incoming call costs £4.80. I know that this is not a very scientific or even sustainable statistic but it does help to make the point to your team how important it is to convert each call to a sale.

Train employees

No one should be permitted to answer the phone until they have had training. This is not a silly point: the way that the phone is answered says so much about your hotel that you cannot leave it to chance. The sound of the voice and the words that are said are vital to making that first impression. Always mention the name of the hotel and who is answering the phone: this introduction gives callers a chance to prepare themselves.

You need to develop a script that takes the customer through the process, and then practise it so that it doesn't sound like you have one. This script should include:

- their name;
- telephone number;
- how they heard about you;
- how many people in their party;

- what their arrival date is;
- what their departure date is;
- what facilities they are looking for;
- list of your main benefits;
- prices and rates;
- their e-mail address for confirmation;
- guarantee/deposit arrangements.

Whatever you do, stick to the scheme that you work out and don't get diverted by customers making the running. You really do need this information and you must provoke a discussion about their needs before you talk about prices. Don't forget to keep checking that your hotel meets their needs by questions such as, 'Does this sound like the sort of service you would enjoy?'

It is also highly professional and certainly less confusing in messages if everyone learns and uses the NATO phonetic alphabet. O for Oscar sounds a lot better than O for Onion or whatever might come into their head at the last moment!

Get information

Even if the caller is not looking for a room reservation you must get contact information from them. If they are a current customer you need to update your records. If they are a new prospect then you need full contact details including name and address and e-mail. To get these, you could offer to send them something (e.g. a voucher for free wine with dinner) by post or e-mail.

Listen carefully

Your phone rings because a prospect wants something. You need to give them what they want but you can't find out what that is unless you listen very carefully. Let them do 80 per cent of the talking.

Ask questions

Ask open-ended questions beginning with what, why and when. Wait for a response and then tailor your next question. If the caller identifies some problem they have (e.g. a bad back) you have a great opportunity to mention your orthopaedic mattresses.

The most difficult call to handle is someone who just asks your price, particularly if they do not know your hotel. If you give it to them you have undermined your ability to compete on value. You need to again ask open-ended questions such 'What type of room are you looking for? or 'What type of features are you expecting for your weekend break?' Any question that allows you to establish your value proposition.

If a caller is ringing in response to an advertisement you could ask open-ended questions such as 'What caught your eye in the ad?' or 'What prompted your call?' Or any question to start a dialogue and show that you are interested on their response.

Automation

The hospitality business is a people business, so I would never recommend an automated answering service. However, if you can't or don't answer the phone 24/7 make sure that you have a good message-taking service. This can either be a machine that you control or a divert service with operator response. If you go the answer machine route, do make sure that the message is really upbeat and enthusiastic and that you do respond just as quickly as you can.

Outgoing calls

We have said that the telephone is a powerful tool, but don't try to get it to do too much. Limit your objectives and you will feel more successful. There are around 220 days in the year when you can make calls. Just one a day can make a difference.

The number of calls you need to make depends on the size of your hotel, the needs of the business, the potential room nights/ meetings from each client and the number of calls you need to make to generate a client.

Reason why

Be very clear about what you are trying to achieve. If you are calling a prospective corporate account it is highly unlikely that you are going to generate room nights from the call (they don't know you, they haven't seen the product, they are quite happy etc): it is just the start of a relationship.

The reason for your first call is only research to find out the right person to contact. Your second call is to see if they are interested in your hotel as a potential supplier. Your third call is to invite them to view your hotel or for you to visit them. And so on as the relationship develops.

Be prepared

Always be prepared. Look at the company's website, drive by their office so that you can visualise the location and know what they do. You can get some of this information from the 'gatekeeper' or from the internet.

Getting past the gatekeeper

You must always assume that the gatekeeper (any person between you and the prospect) is an important individual, give them respect and try and make them your friend. They are often subject to a lot of hostility so you being nice to them may make a change. The most powerful question to ask a gatekeeper is 'please can you help me?' Always take the opportunity to acknowledge the importance of the gatekeeper. Keep your introduction short and ask to speak to your contact. If you have sent a letter prior to your call you can claim to be following up a sort of 'relationship'.

If the target is unavailable, you need to find out the best time to call and then when you call back you can say 'Hi, you said I should call back …'. Always assume that no one will call back and you won't be disappointed.

Dealing with rejection

There really is no such thing! Not every organisation you contact will be in the market for what you offer; this is just the nature of business. The phone is the tool you are using for qualifying prospects. You are evaluating their business potential and then deciding whether to go any further. It is not a personal thing that they don't have any potential for your hotel; they are not rejecting your offer they are just saying that it doesn't suit their needs.

Warm or cold calling

There is always a lot of discussion about the value of sending material to a prospect before you call. I have always found that it works best by:

- finding the decision maker by phone;
- sending a brief (no more than one page) introduction letter saying you will call;
- making a follow-up call to make an appointment or whatever.

Cold calling is definitely harder, and by sending something in advance at least you have made a reason to call. If you are calling because you were referred by a mutual contact then that is all the excuse you need. Just mention their name in your call and it is no longer a cold call but a follow-up from a reference.

Ask questions

The most important objective in making a phone call to a prospect is to start a quality conversation about whether or not there is potential for both parties to do business. You can only do this by asking questions, especially those that begin with what, why, when, where, who and how. Make sure you avoid weak questions such as:

- 'I'm just calling to catch up with you.'
- 'I just wanted to see if there was anything you needed.'
- 'I'm calling to introduce my hotel to you.'
- 'I'd like to set up a time for you to visit my hotel.'

You need to open your calls with questions that relate to their objectives, not yours.

Very often the answer to your questions will be, 'We're fine with our current hotel.' This may mean that they are fine or that things could be better. You need to probe a bit to keep the conversation going and to find out the real answer. Try, 'You say things are fine. What service aspects would you improve if you could?' or 'What would prevent you trying an alternative hotel as a one-off experiment?' Remember to keep treating the call as 'research'. Even if they are an unlikely buyer now, you never know when they might need you. It can often take one or two years for a pay-off.

Don't get pushed around

Sometimes you have a high level contact who refers you on to someone else in the organisation that makes the decision about contracts or conferences. This can get very political, particularly when the person you are referred to doesn't respond.

First of all make sure that you ask your contact that it is OK to get back to them with the result of your conversation with the decision maker: this is your route back. Then tell the decision maker (by voice mail if necessary) that you said that you would get back to your contact with the outcome by a specific day. This way you are fulfilling a promise, not telling tales.

Effective telephone techniques

- Speak very clearly; match your voice to the recipient.
- Sound really positive.
- Don't accept offers to 'call you back'.
- Stand up to call; it can make you feel more in control.
- Smile all the time; you really can hear it.

- Visualise looking the person in the eye.
- When the other person is talking, make encouraging comments.
- Use a headset; it allows you to make your usual gestures.
- Don't eat or drink (or tap your pen); the sound travels.
- Make notes beforehand; be ready for anything.

DIRECT CONTACT

I could have titled this section 'direct sales'. But this might have put you off. Who wants to read anything about such a harsh, unfriendly activity as sales? What indeed is 'sales'?

Poor sales practitioners have unfortunately sullied the reputation of the sales business: we can all imagine the door-to-door salesman, foot in door, foisting their unwanted goods on unsuspecting householders. It is not all like this. Indeed, I would contend that there is no such thing as selling; there is only giving people the opportunity to buy.

What we are doing in the hotel business, with our range of hospitality options, is helping people, not selling. We are helping our contacts to meet their objectives, whether they are a booker trying to give her overnight visitors a relaxing overnight stay or a meeting planner with a brief to provide a creative environment. It is a collaborative process, leading to a mutually satisfactory outcome.

◆ TIP ◆

If you can keep in your mind that you are helping, then the task of communicating with your prospects can become a pleasure rather than a chore.

There are some extremely helpful sales and catering software systems available that enable you to track business sources and file revenue generated by company. You can also send proposals straight to your prospect's computer. However we are still in the people business and must not let the technology blind us to the need to develop rapport with prospects and clients by meeting them face to face either at their offices or on-site. This is not only a job for your sales executive (if you have one), but for others too.

Be prepared

The process upon which you are about to embark begins with the customer, not your product. Always prepare thoroughly because you will need some edge in your discussion and this may be the way to gain it. Do a Google search on the company (and the person you are seeing) and find out what they sell or do, what their competition is, how profitable they are and who owns them.

Think about why you are making this visit or having this meeting. You must never sit down with a prospect unless you have some written objectives plus an idea of some of the questions you will ask. What do you want to achieve from the meeting? Is it an order, or an appointment for them to visit you?

It is helpful to prepare some cue cards for yourself, highlighting your features and benefits and any other company or personal information you have gathered. An agenda is also helpful, even if you don't give it to your prospect. Just having it will keep you on track.

Use your personality

However great your hotel and its food, most people are buying into a relationship with you, not the physical product. If you want to be remembered, do whatever you can to be different, but in a memorable way. Discover your uniqueness. I don't mean that you should wear a silly hat, but let your personality shine through. Think about the way you dress and the way that you talk to people.

Think of ways that you add value to your relationships by sending birthday cards, hand-written notes with articles of interest etc. Always display a positive attitude and have your best smile on your face. If you can be different, then great.

Your prospects also have differing personalities. Extroverts are sociable, active and impulsive. Introverts are less sociable, less active and more cautious. Their behaviour will mirror their personality; if an extrovert says, 'I'll think about it' it probably means 'No'! Adjust your approach depending on your prospect.

Problems and opportunities

Your main objective is to get to some understanding about your prospect's problems, needs and desires. It is best to start with questions around these issues. It is tempting to feel you ought to start with some more general questions about his golf handicap, but how do you help him with this? Be guided by the prospect. Wait for him to start.

Identify all the specific problems he has; this will give you the opportunity to incorporate your solutions into your presentation.

Ask questions

The key to any successful contact with a prospect is the quality of your questions. Good questions receive good, useful and illuminating answers. The reverse is also true. Always keep questions short, use 'you' a lot, and keep them open-ended.

Ask your questions clearly, match the tone of voice to your contact and wait for the answer. Respect the silence. It is also very helpful to write down your questions before the meeting so that they are not a surprise to you. This way you will be able to organise your questions around the outcome that you want. Preparing in advance also gives your subconscious the opportunity to help you.

Although you should usually use open-ended questions (starting with who, what, why, when and how) there are times when you just want a straight one-word answer. Here are some really powerful questions. You don't have to use them all, and you will have some of your own.

General business questions to find out context:

♦ 'Tell me about your business.'
♦ 'Describe the people in your organisation.'
♦ 'What are your responsibilities?'
♦ 'What are the biggest challenges you face in growing your business?'
♦ 'What are your priorities?'

Moving on to supply issues:

♦ 'What do you like about your current hotel.'

- 'If you could change anything about your current hotel, what would it be?'
- 'What qualities are you looking for in a new hotel?'
- 'What are your criteria for making a decision?'
- 'Under what circumstances would you use a new hotel?'
- 'What is your decision-making process?'
- 'How do you measure the success of your current hotel?'
- 'What are your expectations from a new hotel?'
- 'When do you decide on new hotel contracts?'
- 'How many room nights do you book each month?'
- 'What do you know about my hotel?'

Try to avoid soft, bland questions:

- 'How are you?'
- 'Can I be honest?'
- 'I was wondering…'
- 'Yes, I agree, but…'
- 'I may be wrong but…'
- 'I see your point, but…'

Active listening

Whatever you do, listen to the answer. Don't just plough on with your own agenda regardless. By all means keep your objective in mind but it might not be a straight line from beginning to end. Just to show that you are listening, try asking, 'Am I right in thinking that what you are saying is…?'

Listening is the key to navigating your way through the relationship so that you achieve what you want. Listen for the silences and the pauses and don't immediately jump in with another question. Don't hurry the conversation along or be rushed into speaking.

 TIP

> Always listen twice as much as you talk and you will find out all
> that you need to know; if you don't know what they really want,
> how can you offer them a solution?

Listen closely enough to take notes and where possible write down some quotes that you can use later in your presentation. Speak to any police officer and they will tell you that when a suspect is talking they don't do or say anything that makes them stop. This is definitely worth bearing in mind for your prospects.

Very often sales are lost (particularly for meetings) by not making the correct offer. This is caused by not understanding your prospects' real needs. If there is anything you don't understand ask for clarification and then summarise your perception before moving on. If you have been in the same sales situation before, and can almost predict the requirements, avoid being too quick. Appear thoughtful and the customer will see that you have come up with a solution that is tailor made for their particular situation.

Effective negotiation

It would be great if you didn't have to negotiate, but if you deal with corporate accounts it is most likely that they will not be happy unless they have achieved some 'concession' (it makes them feel good!). The outcome must be to the ultimate benefit of both parties. The challenge is to sign the business without giving something away that compromises other business opportunities or relationships. What you must never do is discount your rates without negotiating to get more room nights than you would have done at the higher price.

The best tactic is preparation. If you know what the negotiating points are, then work out your lowest position on all aspects of the prospective deal and stick to them. If a corporate account wants a lower price then maybe agree, but only give the difference as a retrospective discount after producing an agreed number of room nights each year. If a conference organiser wants a lower overall package rate then try to negotiate on the payment terms.

Overcoming resistance

It is most likely that you will come up against some resistance to your offers. Often objections are thrown up by the buyer just to convince themselves that you can meet their needs. Think of resistance as a positive issue. If a client does not have any, they are an unlikely buyer. No one bothers to object to a proposal that leaves them totally unimpressed.

Ideally you will have incorporated into your presentation objections that you have heard before. Make sure that you give your prospect time to digest them. Don't rush through; take time to recap and then move on.

If price is thrown up as an area of resistance then you need very quickly to stop talking 'price' and talk 'investment'. This works well with business prospects, since most of them are in the business of investing for the future. Overnight accommodation for their executives may well be a cost but if you can set out all the benefits of this investment (particularly against their current supplier) then you may well deflect the discussion!

If your prospect says 'What are your rates?' too early (before your presentation), answer 'It depends'. You can then set out all the things that it depends on, such as the number of room nights, when their demand is, what meals are needed, how much credit they want etc. Then you can steer the conversation back on track.

One of the most difficult objections is when your prospect says that they will think it over. To find out whether or not this is just their way of saying no, you need to explore exactly what it is that they want to think about.

Ask them to specify whether it is the menu, the facilities, the perceived value or whatever. Once you have isolated their issue you can ask, 'Is that the only thing that is stopping you going ahead now?' If you receive a positive response you can go over the issue again. Once you leave their office or they leave your hotel it is extremely unlikely they will spend any time thinking it over.

The main difficulty in dealing with objections is sorting the fundamental from the spurious. Only experience will guide you in dealing with them seriously or deflecting them.

Making proposals

Sometimes you will be asked to submit a written proposal. This may be after you have gained a commitment, it could be as an interim stage before another meeting or it could be because there is more than one decision maker. Your letter should include these paragraphs:

- Restatement of what you are quoting for.
- Your understanding of what the client wants to achieve.
- Summary of benefits of your hotel (for this specific quote).
- Prices, rates, timescale and any conditions.
- Hotel contacts.

Your next step will depend on the circumstances. If the proposal is just the next stage of the process, include a second copy for the client to sign and return.

Gaining commitment

Your ultimate objective is to get a buying decision. You can only ask for a positive decision if you have aroused enough desire on the part of your prospect and satisfied all his objections. A perfect process, where you have completely understood the customer's problems and made a perfect presentation, will lead to a buying decision, but this rarely happens. Whatever you do though, make sure you actually ask for their commitment. Try:

- 'We seem to be in agreement. What would you like the next step to be?'

- 'If I could take care of that concern, would you confirm your request today?'

♦ 'It seems that you have made up your mind to do this. Is that right?'

A prospect usually resists making a buying decision. There are usually some negative aspects to a change (like telling the current supplier, who he plays golf with!) so he needs help or incentives to make the decision.

There are a number of ways to create the right circumstances for a buying decision:

♦ **Offer alternatives**: 'Would you like the small or the large meeting room?'

♦ **Review benefits.**

♦ **Aim at part decisions**: 'Why not start by booking just the sales manager in to an executive room to see how she likes the hotel?'

♦ **Tailor offer perfectly**: 'OK, I will order in that champagne specially for you.'

♦ **Let prospect try product**: 'Just so that you can be sure, would you like to book in your next visitor on a complimentary basis?'

♦ **Review objections.**

♦ **Assume the order**: 'When you have booked in the next sales executive, let's have a short meeting to review her comments.'

If you feel that you have done everything right and you still can't get a decision then it is time to be brutal. Ask: 'If this is a good idea we should go ahead, but if it isn't then we should forget about it. Which is it?'

There are plenty of books on 'closing techniques' but if your prospect has read the same book they will not appreciate being 'techniqued'!

Using technology

Effective use of new technology can transform the amount of proposals and follow up. Whether you have specialist sales staff or not, it is vital that you consider the whole sales process – locating new prospects, qualifying and closing, sending out brochures and proposals and effective communication with prospects and clients. Analyse where the effective use of technology could save you time and speed up your response.

Obviously your scale of operation has an impact on what technology you need. However whether you have five or 500 rooms you still need to keep comprehensive details of your clients and prospects. At some stage contact management software becomes useful, particularly if you are doing e-marketing campaigns to specific market segments.

If you are trying for trade show business then mailing an e-postcard is definitely beneficial. If you are doing a lot of information and brochure fulfilment, your stationery needs to be on your computer so that correspondence can be sent electronically.

 TIP

Your information is your lifeblood. It doesn't matter whether you keep it on a database or sheets of A4 paper.

Handling complaints

During your dealings with corporate bookers you may well receive complaints. Clients complain for a variety of different reasons, some justified and some not. Whatever the reason, you must listen, apologise (for the problem or the fact that they have had to complain) and agree a course of action. Remember that, if handled well, a complaining guest can become a loyal customer. The difficulty with intermediaries is that you receive the comments second hand, so you have to make both the booker and the guest happy.

Even if unjustified, it is wise to let the customer appear to be right. There is no credit in pursuing a long argument that proves you right and the guest wrong: he will still bad-mouth you. Far better to get the reputation for standing behind your product and owning up when things go wrong. Be generous and the customer will feel well treated and tell his friends.

If you receive written complaints, try to avoid a point-by-point correspondence. It never achieves anything except an escalation, which may well end up with lawyers. Act quickly, pick up the phone and do something different; a bunch of flowers really can soothe ruffled feathers!

Body language

In any situation we pick up meaning from a number of different sources. We listen to the words and the tone of voice and we pick up signals from how people use their bodies, both voluntarily and involuntarily. Sometimes the most telling expressions of how we feel are involuntary facial signals. All these signals add up to a positive or a negative view of where we are in the sales process.

If you have made your presentation and your prospect seems a bit bored, and is sitting with his arms crossed then it would be sensible to assume that he is not yet ready to make a decision in your favour. We are looking for a person's body language to confirm what we hear.

Much of our current thinking on body language stems from studies made by Professor Albert Mehrabian in 1971. He concluded that there are three parts to any face-to-face communication:

◆ words
◆ tone of voice
◆ body language.

These three elements account differently for the meaning of the message: words account for 7 per cent, tone of voice accounts for 38 per cent and body language accounts for 55 per cent of the message. For effective and meaningful communication, these three elements of the message need to be 'congruent'.

Imagine someone says to you, 'I do not have a problem with you,' but at the same time they avoid eye contact, look anxious and fold their arms. Because of the incongruence between the verbal and the non-verbal, you would naturally tend to put more emphasis on the non-verbal communication (55 per cent) rather than hearing the actual words spoken.

This study was based on experiments dealing with communicating likes and dislikes. The disproportionate influence of tone of voice and body language only becomes effective when the situation is ambiguous. This does not mean that in every situation body language is so predominant. However there are some aspects of body language that can be helpful in indicating what the subconscious intentions are behind certain actions.

It is also useful to appreciate that where we don't have the opportunity to convey or reinforce meaning by our body language we have to be more careful.

◆ TIP ◆

Writing a memo or e-mail can easily convey an unintended message if we are not very careful about the words and the 'tone' we use.

This lack of body signals is one reason why telephone conversations are sometimes quite difficult, particularly for sensitive or emotional issues.

What to look for

+ **Leaning towards you**: comfortable in your company or interested in what you are saying.

+ **Leaning away from you**: the opposite of the above. If they start to support their head on the hand then you'd better think of something quickly or they'll soon be asleep!

+ **Crossed legs or arms**: defensive or negative or just don't like what you are saying. This is the time to hand them a brochure so that they have to uncross their arms.

+ **Fingers together forming a steeple**: feel superior and may be preparing to give you a lecture, so get ready.

◆ **Hand over mouth while *you* are talking:** either they think you are lying or they do not like what is being said. They might also just want their turn to speak.

◆ **Hand over mouth while *they* are talking:** they might just be nervous or they could actually be lying.

◆ **Closed hand on cheek, chin stroking, polishing glasses:** evaluating and decision making indicators. You are going in the right direction and you should keep going to the end.

◆ **Smiling and changing their body position to lean towards you and be more open:** all indicators that the 'yes' is about to come.

Look in their eyes

Each half of our brain deals with different types of data. The right half processes intangible and creative elements. The left half processes logic and academic thought. As we use our brain our eyes move and it is this movement that give us information about others' thought processes. These indicators take some practice, particularly if you want to be unobtrusive.

◆ A right-handed person looking up and to the left is accessing visual memory. They look up and to the right to create mind pictures; to the left ear to access sound memory and to the right to create sound. This is a bit tricky since some left-handed people work the opposite way round and some don't!

◆ The position of the upper eyelid is a good indicator of the level of interest; the higher the eyelid the more the interest.

◆ The red triangle in the corner of your eye is called the inner canthus. When this is covered the customer is showing concern and you cannot ask for the order yet. When you can see the inner canthus then you are getting somewhere and their interest level is raised.

What you can do

♦ You should show leadership and confidence by sitting upright. Keep looking ahead (without staring), and make eye contact for about five seconds at a time, placing your hands in a steeple position and not smiling too much.

♦ You can request feedback to a question you have asked by putting out your right hand, palm up and about six inches in front of you. This gesture clearly shows that you are handing the conversation over to the other person.

♦ You can change your own position by either standing up or moving around. This may prompt the customer to change also.

♦ Match the speed, pressure and time of a handshake and maintain eye contact. This indicates that you consider the relationship to be equal.

♦ If you notice some negative body behaviour, try asking some short questions that just need the answer 'yes'. You should notice a change to a more positive attitude.

First impressions

The first few seconds

Much has been written about first impressions, which count a lot not only in sales and networking situations but also in job interviews. Whenever I have interviewed job applicants I have always made a conscious effort to put my first impression to one side and give potential applicants the benefit of a well-structured interview. But maybe I shouldn't have given myself such a hard time: recent research has shown that a teacher whose effectiveness was evaluated by his students over a whole term got the same reaction from students who only watched five seconds of the same teacher on video!

What happens next?

A first impression is made up of two elements. First, within a few seconds we perform what psychologists call a 'thin slice'. Malcolm Gladwell, in his book *Blink*, defines this as 'the innate human ability to be able to get to the truth of someone or something in an instant.' During this initial activity our subconscious picks up all the non-verbal clues: checking out clothes, look, expressions, walk, height etc. We get to the truth as we see it, based of course on our prevailing attitudes and prejudices.

Second, we move onto interacting with the other person, making new and generally more conscious evaluations over the next ten minutes or so. This first impression tends to last a long time and whenever we speak to the same person again we tend to try to look for information that will confirm our first impression.

Prejudices

It is very useful to be aware of your own prejudices, whether these are about race, height, accent or gender. If you know that you have a particular prejudice against say, a certain regional accent, then you need to spend the few minutes after the 'thin slice' trying to make a personal connection with the other person.

An interview is a relatively structured situation and you know that you should try to get the interviewee to talk – you know you have to give them an opportunity to sell themselves. In other less formal situations there are some tactics that you can employ to try to ensure that you give a good first impression. Above all, show genuine interest in the other person and you will be seen as having a generous spirit.

Tips for making a good first impression

◆ **Start with a strong handshake** – you are seen as more confident, assertive and intelligent. It is particularly vital for women to avoid the 'wet fish' approach but also don't try to dominate with a 'bone crusher'.

◆ **Don't disclose too much personal information too soon** – you can appear too self-absorbed.

◆ **Stay relaxed** – it makes you seem approachable. Smiling too much appears fake but not smiling looks cold.

◆ **Think about your clothes** – people who wear a bit of colour are seen to be more accessible than those who wear severe clothes in dark colours.

◆ **Stay positive** – even if you have had a dreadful journey, starting a conversation with a negative makes you seem difficult.

◆ **Show you're pleased to meet someone** – be enthusiastic, smile and try to connect with what is being said. We all like people who like us.

◆ **Try to start the conversation** – whoever starts the conversation gains an element of gratitude from the other person.

- ◆ **Listen carefully** – don't interrupt. Stay focused on the other person, be genuinely interested and make occasional appreciative comments.

- ◆ **You don't need to talk** – and if while listening you smile, lean forward and look at the talker, you will make a positive impression.

- ◆ **Let others talk** – good first impressions are made by encouraging others to talk about themselves, not by you showing off your talents or achievements.

- ◆ **Share the conversation** – try to speak for less than 50 per cent of the time and don't always try to steer the conversation back to your experiences.

NETWORKING

For the owner of any sort of hotel, networking can be powerful as you are in direct contact with local people who might be users, bookers or recommenders. Most of the contacts will be people who know people, and over time this sort of referral will produce results. Of course it is possible to waste your time, but if you choose the network club or association carefully you can generate measurable results.

Maybe your hotel can become the venue for a lunch club, either regularly or occasionally. Some networks (particularly BNI) meet for breakfast (very early) but being the venue does show off your location even though you may not feel at your best!

Even when dealing with large organisations, people are still buying from people and they only buy from people they know, like and trust.

Networking is a great environment because it is designed to help you get to know people first. Don't forget that everyone at the event has the same objective.

Making the most of networking events

- Find out who else will be there so you are prepared.
- Set yourself a goal for how many people you will talk to.
- Find out the purpose of the event.
- Have a 60-second summary ready for 'And what do you do?'
- Always be positive.
- Take some brochures if a display table is part of the format.
- Look the part and be memorable.
- Introduce yourself to as many new people as possible.
- Move on politely when the conversation ends (maximum ten minutes).
- Try to remember names.
- Postpone all sales opportunities for later follow up.
- Take your own name badge if none supplied.
- Take plenty of business cards or maybe special offers.
- Don't give your business card unless it is asked for.
- Attend regularly and only evaluate after 12 months.
- Always follow up contacts made.
- If you get a referral make sure you thank the person.

Useful questions

A networking event is a bit like the start of a sales call. The important difference is that you don't move on to make your presentation! What you are trying to do is find out as much as you can about the person you are talking to. Try something like this:

- How did you get into the _____ business?

- What is the most enjoyable part of the _____ business?

- How do you separate yourself from the competition?

- Has the _____ business changed much over the last few years?

- Do you find it difficult to recruit new staff?

- What changes do you expect in the future?

- What are the most effective ways to promote your business?

KEY POINTS

- If you know the names of prospects then telephone and personal meetings are the most effective ways of starting to build relationships.

- The telephone is a powerful tool but not everyone is naturally effective at using it. No one should answer incoming calls without training and role-playing exercises.

- Whenever you are in direct contact with prospects you should listen for twice as much time as you speak.

- The most effective outcomes from direct selling are achieved by thorough preparation and good questions.

- Networking can be effective if you attend the right events and treat it as work.

5

Direct Marketing

Direct marketing can be an extremely effective way to deliver your message to your prospects. It is different to advertising, in that the messages are delivered to named individuals. Of course, like most activities, you can do it well or you can do it badly. Much of the problems with direct marketing are associated with choosing your targets badly. New technology has created new opportunities such as e-mail, SMS and interactive TV.

DIRECT MAIL

Direct mail has developed something of a poor reputation. This is mostly associated with our own personal experience of being sent inappropriate mailings that go straight into the bin. It also seems to be the height of extravagance when an agency intimates that if you get more than a one per cent response it will be a success!

So how do you get a better response? How can you avoid being 'junk' mail?

Power of direct mail

The power of direct mail is in the word 'direct'. It enables you to directly target a number of prospects and deliver your message direct to them. It is not as precise as direct sales but it is much more targeted than advertising. The benefit is in the numbers. It is an invaluable way of getting the attention of a large number of targets at the same time with the same message, while you are off doing something else.

Response usually peaks within a couple of weeks and you can then accurately measure the profitability of the campaign.

Costs

Costs can be kept low. It is possible to send a complete mailing at the minimum postage rate for around 50 pence if you just use one A4 page plus a cheap envelope and do the complete mailing yourself. If you use postcards it can be even less. Costs can increase dramatically if you have to rent a list or you use an outside agency.

The right target

The success of any direct mail activity depends on the quality of the list. Your list must be of people that are going to be interested in your offer. If you are promoting your restaurant then the prospects must live within a certain distance. If you are trying to develop interest in your new meeting room then your named list must be contacts that actually book meeting rooms. This seems very obvious but sometimes the appropriateness gets lost along the way.

If you are mailing to your own list it is relatively easy to keep the offer appropriate. What you need is a database that enables you to highlight exactly what your customers are interested in. Not all your business users will be interested in your Christmas package. Your previous overnight guests from 300 miles away will not be interested in your new lunch menu!

If you are buying a list you have to be more careful in specifying exactly what customers you are targeting.

List making

Buying in lists from outside your hotel can be effective. For instance, if you are trying to promote your weekend packages you could obtain a list of people who have previously bought such a product from elsewhere. Here you need to check how closely your product matches the product they have previously bought.

You could alternatively ask a list broker to put together a list of likely purchasers based on some demographic, psychographic or geographic parameters that you supply, based on your experience of your previous guests. Of course, for this to work effectively, you need to gather the same sort of information on your current users.

Often the company data kept by a hotel is not very accurate. No contact is very useful unless you have the correct contact name, company name and complete postcode. As with consumers, business data changes very frequently. Dun and Bradstreet reckon that seven per cent of businesses move each year and if you add in contact moves and promotions there can be some sort of change in company data of up to five per cent per month.

There are many sources of business data, but you need to work with a company that takes note of your current data and activity and builds a list of prospects with you. Avoid organisations that just want to sell you a list.

Sequential mailings

Depending on how much you expect new customers to spend over their lifetime with you, it is likely to be beneficial to do more than one mailing in a series, the second about two weeks after the first. This is an effective way of maximising your list. Each mailing needs to be worked out in advance so that there is a link between them all. They must look similar and be promoting the same service.

The only difficulty is taking out of each subsequent mailing those targets that have already responded. If you use contact management software it is relatively simple but otherwise you will need to set up some in-house mechanism.

◆ TIP ◆

Be careful if you are using a rented list: there is usually a restriction on how many times you can use each address.

Also be careful about sticking to the conditions on which you rented the list; the owner of the list will have put some 'check' addresses within the list so that they receive copies of your mailing. Once you convert the target to a user then the contact is yours.

Get your letter opened

The first hurdle is actually getting your envelope opened. Perhaps this is why postcards can be so effective! No one likes to be misled by mailings that look like they are from the government. However research does indicate that the more like personal mail you can make it the better. Ideally you will hand write the envelopes and stick on stamps. If this is too much, try not to compromise too far – typewritten addresses are OK but stick with the stamp. Also remember that most people open direct mail letters while standing over the waste paper basket.

Do you need a gimmick?

Interesting question. Grabbing your target's attention is the most difficult task so anything that makes them open the letter must be a help. If you are promoting a new spa facility then a sachet of shower gel in the envelope will be intriguing. On the other hand, I don't think the very cheap pens in charity mailings work any more.

There is much anecdotal evidence to suggest that so-called 'lumpy' mail is more likely to be opened. There are lots of things you can use from seed packets to CDs. Whatever you do make the insert appropriate to your message. If you are sending a mailing to a corporate list, many executives (particularly those that are field based) have an assistant who opens their post so something appropriate for this gatekeeper can work well.

Copywriting

Once you have managed to have your envelope opened there is still the challenge to have your letter read. People read these unsolicited letters in what might seem a random order. First they read the top and the headline to get the gist of what it is about and what organisation it is from. Secondly they read the PS and thirdly they read the sub-headings to see if they throw any more light on the subject. If they are still with you they might then read the rest of the letter, so long as the first sentence grabs them. Quite a challenge!

According to direct marketing legend Drayton Bird there are fewer and fewer really good copywriters around and you probably cannot afford those that are any good. However if you are asking someone else to write for you ensure that their letter follows some of the following guidelines.

If you are only sending an introductory letter, your letter must be on one side of paper and needs to be read and understood in 30 seconds. Use short paragraphs and bullet points. For any other letter the length really doesn't matter. What is vital is to make it interesting. David Ogilvy claimed that you couldn't bore people into buying. If what you are saying is exciting, amusing and of definite interest you can develop your argument over any number of pages.

Headline

The first item to get right in your letter is the headline. It must grab your reader's attention and intrigue them enough to continue. There are a number of traditional headline formats that seem to work in most situations:

How to ...
5 reasons to join our new Spa.

7 reasons to try our new restaurant.
Introducing a new way to save money.
Now ...
At Last ...
Guaranteed ...
Free ....
Special half price offer.

Of course you can develop your own as well.

Body copy

There is a very useful structure for organising any direct mail letter. It has worked forever so there is no reason why it can't work for you. Just remember **AIDA** (some people use AIDCA, which splits the procedure differently, but the effect is the same):

Attention – through the first line in the body copy (makes me want to read further).

Interest – by setting out the benefits (this seems relevant to me or my company).

Desire – by overcoming their scepticism (this could be of real benefit to me).

Action – what do you want the reader to do next? (I'll take the follow-up call or send off the reply, whatever).

Attention: The first thing you need to do to get anyone to read your letter is grab people's attention. You do this with a compelling first sentence. If this doesn't grab attention the rest of the letter will never be read at all. Spend most of your time on the sentence and make it one of the following:

- Benefit-driven: 'You can ...'
- News-orientated: 'Great new ...'
- Curiosity-driven: 'Are you ...?'
- How-to orientated: 'How to ...'

Don't make them too long (about ten short words work best). Think of at least 20 options and test them on your staff and maybe some customers.

Interest: After you have the reader's attention you need to stimulate their interest in your service by explaining the benefits. Address yourself to an individual and their wants and don't talk about your hotel and how good you think you are. Prospects only want to know how your offer can benefit them. And don't confuse them by trying to sell more than one service.

To write really powerful copy you need to understand exactly what it is that motivates your target market. You need to reach them on an emotional, an intellectual and a personal level. Before you can do this you need to find out the emotions, attitudes and aspirations that drive them:

- **Beliefs.** What does your audience believe? What is their attitude towards your hotel or restaurant and the problems it solves?

- **Feelings.** How do they feel? If you are addressing meeting planners, what do they feel about their role in the process. How does their company treat them?

- **Desires.** What do they want from life? What are their goals and what do they want from their leisure time?

Generally people only want one of two things – either to gain pleasure or avoid pain. There can be a lot of pain for meeting planners so explore this before offering your own solutions, using strong and relevant benefits. For weekend guests your copy should be more about pleasure, again using relevant and appropriate benefits (see section on features and benefits in Chapter 2).

Desire: This is where you need to convert the prospect's interest into a specific desire for your offer. The best way to do this is to overcome the consumer's natural scepticism about claims or offers. Use a selection of these tactics and you will reduce the risk to the consumer:

♦ *Testimonials*
   Consumers like to know that other people have been there before and were happy. For a local market it can be really effective to include a testimonial from someone well known, particularly if you can use their picture.

♦ *Guarantee*
   If your prospect likes your offer and there is no risk because you are guaranteeing satisfaction, what has he got to lose? Why would you not be prepared to stand behind your service? If you aren't prepared to, then maybe you should think about improving the offer.

   Guarantees work really well when you are trying to get corporate or conference buyers to use you for the first time. Time guarantees for lunch are also popular and can help to keep your chefs on their toes.

◆ *Awards*

Although this is very much talking about yourself, it can give consumers confidence if they know that you have an award or have been inspected by a well-known organisation and achieved a high quality score. This is why Michelin Stars are so coveted.

Action: This is one of the most crucial aspects of your letter. If all the other phases go well and there is no action, then you have failed. You must say exactly what you want readers to do. 'Call now,' or 'Visit our website now' are the final triggers that enable prospects to take action on an offer that they have been stimulated by.

If you are including an order form then make it easy to send back. Have the name and address of the customer already completed and include on the form most of the salient points, just in case the form becomes separated from the mailing.

It can sometimes help to introduce an element of scarcity. 'First come, first served' or 'Free to the first 50 callers' can be very powerful incentives. It is particularly useful in special offers that are available for a limited period: 'Special lunch price only available until 30 April.'

Post Script (PS)
Here you need to restate the offer very succinctly. Add a PPS also if you think it will help.

Checklist
◆ Use short paragraphs.
◆ Don't use industry jargon.

- No sentence longer than 25 words.
- Use short, warm words.
- Focus on benefits, not features.
- Write like a personal conversation.
- Keep it simple.
- Don't criticise competition.
- Use positives rather than negatives.
- Always use 'you' and 'your' rather than 'I' and 'we'.
- Use bullet points.
- Check spelling and grammar.
- Have someone else check-read the letter.
- Would you be happy to receive the proposition?

Measuring success

First of all you need to decide what you consider to be success. Ultimately you need profit from the exercise but over what period? Set yourself a target and measure it. Look at responses and then figure who actually made a booking for a room or a restaurant reservation.

If the lifetime value of a restaurant customer is £1,500 (£150 per annum for 10 years) and you acquire 70 new customers from a mailing to 1,500 prospects that cost £1,500 you would be very happy. If you only found eight new customers you would be disappointed.

E-MAIL

The benefit of e-mail is that it is a 'free' service. This is also its main drawback. As everyone knows, anyone can send e-mail to anyone which makes it a breeding ground for 'spam'!

Interestingly, we seem to be moving away from spam as the main issue. There are plenty of spam filters available and most people seem to be able to delete and move on.

However it is no longer enough to have permission through an opt-in. Everyone has given out a lot of permissions so now the challenge is, as with direct mail, to get your message delivered and read. Well planned and executed e-mail campaigns can achieve a delivery rate of 90 per cent, with around 40 per cent of delivered messages opened and ten per cent clicked through. Some commentators claim that most people regularly open and read 16 permission-based e-mails. To get yours read you have to displace one of these and enter that 'inner-circle' of trusted senders. You have to make your message seem interesting enough to open.

Personalise

One tactic is to put the prospect's name in the subject field. This shows up as a potential personal message and seems to have an influence on the likelihood of the message being opened. If you are opening a new restaurant, then you could put the following as the subject: 'David, here's your free invitation.' On the other hand do you ever receive personal mail with your name in the subject line? As with most aspects of the internet some things work for a time and then the opposite takes effect. Just try different tactics and see what works.

Entice

Personalising is important but you still need to let your prospects know exactly what is in it for them. You need the reader to be curious and see quickly what benefits there are for them. By putting a clear benefit in the subject line you will be letting your customers know how your service will improve their lives.

But you need to be succinct. Your subject line can only be about 40 characters long both because of the limits of the subject line space and also because any longer and the e-mail stands less chance of being opened at all.

You need very quickly to convince your busy prospects that your message is worthy of attention. Subject lines should be one of the following:

♦ **Urgent.** This gives the reader a reason to act now instead of later. Include a time-limited offer such as 'special offer if booked by tomorrow'.

♦ **Unique.** Even if readers have heard it before, say it in a unique way. 'Why our Spa guests look radiant.'

♦ **Ultra-specific.** These can tease the reader into opening your e-mail. 'What never to do at your wedding.'

♦ **Useful.** Needs to offer a benefit. 'Now WiFi for your guests.'

When you have written your subject line, test how strong it is against all four 'U's above. Score it out of five and make sure that it rates at least a three or four in at least three 'U's.

Whatever you do, don't write copy that is different to the subject line. It is probably illegal and certainly breaks trust with your customer.

Keep it short

E-mail is not the vehicle for long messages. Of course an e-zine is a different proposition, which is covered later. Long e-mails are hard to read and they are best kept to as few words as possible. If you have a longer message it is quite acceptable to provide a link to a website that can be instantly accessed for a benefit.

How often?

There is no hard and fixed rule about how often you can make contact by e-mail. So long as you have permission from the recipient, you can e-mail every day if you have something that is of use and is relevant. You can send me a voucher for a free meal or extra frequent flyer miles every day if you wish! But if you do the same to sell me printer cartridges I will unsubscribe very quickly.

Relevant

As with any direct marketing media, it is a complete waste of time if you do not reach your target. You must tailor your message to your target market. For this you need segmented mailing lists so that you can send them relevant and targeted offers. If someone has signed up for your offers they are likely to have signed up with other hotels. You need to beat the competition by ensuring that your messages are anticipated by your prospects because they know that you will give them relevant offers.

Avoiding spam filters

There is a constant battle between spammers and the developers of spam filters. Your messages will often be caught up in the crossfire. To find out if your e-mail is being caught, sign up for a Hotmail or other free account and include messages to yourself in your mailing as a test.

Don't forget that even though you have not sent 'spam' the recipient can still report it as spam to their ISP. This won't happen so long as you are known and trusted.

Most organisations develop their own unacceptable words and phrases but there are some that never get through:

- Money back
- Make money
- 100 per cent satisfied
- Cards accepted
- SPECIAL PROMOTION
- Order now!

Particularly avoid CAPITALS and excessive punctuation!!!!

Test

The joy of e-mail is that it is relatively easy to test. Split your list into manageable portions and measure the reaction to your subject lines or your offers. You can then change individual parts of your e-mail and test the results.

Be very careful with the 'tone' of your e-mail. Any attempt at humour or sarcasm can easily be misinterpreted.

Interesting subjects

For a hotel there are a few options that can help you get your e-mail messages through to the recipient:

- **Transaction e-mails:** You can attach a promotional message to confirmation e-mails that you send to corporate customers about their room or meeting reservations.

- **Membership e-mails:** Prospects will read e-mails from clubs of which they are members. This works well for dining clubs.

- **Free e-zine:** If your newsletter is valuable and published regularly, anything with your name in the 'from' line will be seen as coming from a trusted source.

NEWSLETTERS

Newsletters are a great way to keep in contact with customers and prospects. You can tell them about new facilities and promote future events. Unfortunately, traditional newsletters can be extremely time consuming to do, with the result that enthusiasm sometimes dies off quickly. More effective is an electronic newsletter or e-zine. They are much simpler to produce, are free to send and can generate a very quick response. As with any direct response mechanism, the list is the key to success.

Objective

Your objectives must be very clear and you need to write the content with these in mind. It is likely that you will want to:

- establish your reputation;
- keep in touch with customers and prospects;
- promote new services;
- drive traffic to your website.

Name and content

Yours will not be the only newsletter received by your contact. Your challenge is to make the newsletter interesting and useful enough to be opened each time it appears in the inbox. A catchy name helps but it is the content that works. You will probably need to consider:

- Personal message from you.
- Update on facilities, changes and developments.
- Input from the chef (articles not just recipes).
- Special offers for readers.
- Offers from complementary products (e.g. local shops and spas).
- Local news (e.g. new restaurants, tourist services etc).
- Suggestions and opinions from your customers (offer prizes for good ideas that you adopt).
- Involvement of a local charity.

Keep it relevant

The proliferation of mail, both electronic and snail, as well as the multiplicity of other images, forces us to make our messages relevant. Recipients expect messages customised to their needs. No one has the patience to search for content that is relevant to them; they expect you to do that.

So, no general e-zines to all your market segments. You might send the same e-zine to corporate buyers and meeting planners, but do something different for your weekend guests. This is easy enough so long as you collect and segment the data in the first place.

Make it readable

It is no good if you send out your e-zine and everyone deletes it as soon as it arrives! The recipients of your newsletter are automatically part of a community and it is effective to trade on this. They are the audience and you are the focus so work this to your advantage:

- Develop a personality for the e-zine. Let your personality shine through and people will warm to you.

- Make sure you ask lots of questions or raise issues that persuade people to react.

- Make the contents really useful. Give information that will help people improve their lives. Give tips and suggestions. If you are sending something to meeting planners give them tips on how to negotiate better deals with hotels.

How often?

What you don't want to do is set yourself a target that you can't meet. On the other hand if you send out a newsletter just when you feel like it everyone will have forgotten about you. A regular once-a-month publication is OK and probably suits most hotels. Do stick to the plan and be honest about why you missed the deadline.

It can be helpful to make an outline contents plan for the whole year. You know that there are certain special events throughout the year so develop the plan around these: Christmas/Easter/Mother's Day/Winter Specials etc.

What format?

You can either send the newsletter as text (plain type with no graphics or pictures) or HTML (with graphics and colour). It is easier to write a text version but there are templates that you can buy to help with an HTML version.

There can be some problems with receiving HTML e-zines, which is why most are sent as plain text. To make plain text readable, be careful with the layout. Make the lines no longer than 60 characters, split up the various sections with horizontal lines and spaces, and include great headlines and sub-headlines.

E-mail collection

You will need to be very active to generate a comprehensive mailing list. Offer something of value from your website in return for leaving an e-mail address. You can also give out a small promotional piece with all bills and invoices and have cards on the tables. The key is to demonstrate the value that people will get in return for their address.

Management systems

Ideally you will want to use an internet-based system to manage your e-mail list. You can distribute it from your desktop with the e-zine as an attachment, but hopefully as your list grows you will want to automate the process further.

Eventually you will also want to link your website to your management service so that when people visit your website and leave their e-mail they automatically receive the newsletter.

KEY POINTS

◆ Effective direct mail relies on keeping or acquiring good prospect lists.

◆ Direct mail should only be used to promote your hotel to businesses if there are too many people to talk to directly.

◆ E-mail is an effective channel for promoting your services but there are many pitfalls. You must only communicate things that are definitely of interest to the recipient.

◆ Electronic newsletters are a good way to generate a sense of belonging, particularly if you personalise the contents.

6

Advertising

Advertising can be extremely effective but it has to be done properly. Often it is dismissed as being an ineffective medium but this is usually because the rules have not been followed. The key is in testing to find advertisements that work and measuring their response.

IS ADVERTISING RELEVANT FOR ME?

I guess the first question to ask yourself is, 'Does advertising have a part to play in my armoury?' The answer is a qualified 'Yes, but it depends.' And it depends on whether you make the positive decision to undertake a logical, well thought-out campaign, or you respond to any one of the multitude of phone calls you get everyday offering you a 'fantastic advertising opportunity'.

The answer to these is most definitely, 'No'. The sales executive is only phoning you because they are desperate (you can probably hear all the other desperate sales executives on the phone in the background!). I know it always sounds like a worthy cause but you must stay focused and commercial. Anyway, how are you going to measure the results of a small ad on that free giveaway wall planner or the half page in the police diary?

◆ **TIP** ◆

> For the independent hotel it is vital that if you use advertising, it is not so important that you rely on it to generate all your new leads. It is great for launching new facilities (such as a spa) or introducing new products (such as special theme nights) but after you have been operating for a while you will be relying more on using your database.

The problem with all advertising is making a direct connection with your potential customer. There is so much 'clutter' and everyone is bombarded with so many non-relevant messages that they find it difficult to sort out which messages to view. How do you get people's attention? Anyone involved with TV advertising must be very fed up with hearing how many people use the ad breaks as an excuse to leave the room.

The advent of the internet and the possibilities of pay-per-click advertising have made advertisers focus on ways to replicate this direct approach in the media world. The focus seems to be on the mobile phone, which is seen as the ideal vehicle for reaching identified people with targeted messages. Luckily, to receive the benefit of messages directed straight to us we have to opt-in!

With GPS tracking, it is possible for us to be sent an advertising message just as we are walking or driving past that new restaurant we have been meaning to try.

For the last few years there have been dire predictions about the imminent collapse of conventional advertising. It hasn't happened yet. Indeed there are still new publications being launched on the back of advertisers' demand for more specialist and targeted opportunities. This is really the key. Trying to find small, discrete groups of people with similar lifestyles and then seeing how to reach them. Until we can beam our message to prospects just at the point that they are making a relevant choice we will have to rely on local papers, school and village magazines and specialist magazines.

Is your advertising working?

If you don't know the answer to this, then cancel everything! If you are running advertisements in directories, guides or in local papers and you are not sure about their effectiveness then you really should stop them. If everyone involved in advertising, from the client to the publication, were entirely honest they would admit that much advertising doesn't really work! Remember the childhood story of the emperor's new clothes?

Maybe you are advertising because your competition does. How do you know that it is working for them? Sometimes publications give space away just so that they can tell you that their medium is an ideal vehicle. Be very sceptical about claims from advertising representatives and do talk to your competition: if you all acted together you might save all of you a lot of money. Don't follow the herd.

What type of advertising should you do?

Many publications, particularly trade or specialist ones, are totally supported by hotel chain advertising. It is likely that this is 'image' advertising. The objective for this advertising is often not directly related to business development but to support the franchise. Indeed many hotels have to pay a portion of their revenue to an advertising fund specifically to promote the brand.

As an independent hotel you will very rarely find yourself able to justify such an approach, except maybe in a launch phase. You will be mostly involved in 'direct response', where you can measure the results.

The vital element is to make a clear distinction between the two. Don't try to promote your image and at the same time clutter the advertisement with a coupon. Be very clear about your objective.

Agency or not?

The decision about whether to use an agency or not really depends on how much you spend each year and whether or not you use an agency for your brochures and direct mail. If you follow all the points set out here you can make an effective advertisement yourself and have it produced by the publication. However, I don't feel that you always get the best production job from a publication, and do you really have the time to do everything yourself? Think about the most cost-effective use of your time.

It is probably best to find a good, small agency and use all the information in this chapter to monitor their effectiveness. Be aware of the commission angle. Many small or local publications will negotiate on price direct with you but will not do the same with your agency.

Your target market

Most important is to be clear about your target market. Find out what your target market reads or listens to, when and how they make decisions and how much they are prepared to pay. Consider corporate bookers, weekend guests, conference decision makers, restaurant users, wedding planners and the various ways to reach them. Is there a good publication that could generate some response?

Local papers will often publish in advance a list of the supplements that they have planned. These are great advertising opportunities, but in addition try contacting the editor with any interesting and appropriate stories or offers.

What is your objective?

Be very clear about your objective whenever you sit down to plan an advertisement. Don't confuse your reader: be very specific. Only promote one product and only expect one result. It is often tempting to say to yourself that if you are spending money on an advertisement for your Sunday lunch then you might as well mention your conference facilities and your spa. Don't. You will confuse your reader.

What are you trying to get people to do? Call the hotel, visit personally or visit your website? Make your mind up about the outcome you want and write the whole advertisement with that objective in mind.

Classic rules (AIDA)

The same classic rules apply to advertising as they do to direct mail: **AIDA.**

- Attention – through the headline.
- Interest – by laying out the benefits.
- Desire – by overcoming the reader's natural scepticism.
- Action – what do you want the reader to do next?

Attention

The first thing you need to do is get people's attention. You do this with a compelling headline. This is the most important part of your ad. If your headline doesn't grab attention the rest of the advertisement will never be read at all.

Spend most of your time on the headline and make it one of the following:

- Benefit-driven: 'You can ...'
- News-orientated: 'Great new ...'
- Curiosity-driven: 'Are you ...?'
- How-to orientated: 'How to ...'

Don't make them too long (about ten short words work best). Think of at least 20 options and test them on your staff and maybe some customers.

Once you have your heading, think of a sub-heading to reinforce the message.

Interest

After you have the reader's attention you need to stimulate their interest in your service by explaining the benefits. Address yourself to an individual and their wants and don't talk about your hotel and how good you think you are. Prospects only want to know how your offer can benefit them (see features and benefits in Chapter 2). Generally people only want one of two things – either to gain pleasure or avoid pain.

Desire

This is where you need to convert the prospect's interest into a specific desire for your offer. The best way to do this is to overcome the consumer's natural scepticism about claims or offers from advertisers.

Use a selection of these tactics and you will reduce the risk to the consumer:

Testimonials: Consumers like to know that other people have been there before and were happy. For a local market it can be really effective to include a testimonial from someone well known, particularly if you can use their picture.

Guarantee: If your prospect likes your offer and there is no risk because you are guaranteeing satisfaction, what has he got to lose? Why would you not be prepared to stand behind your service? If you aren't prepared to, then maybe you should think about improving the offer.

Guarantees work really well when you are trying to get corporate or conference buyers to use you for the first time.

Time guarantees for lunch are also popular and can help to keep your chefs on their toes.

Awards: Although this is very much talking about yourself, it can give consumers confidence if they know that you have an award or have been inspected by a well-known organisation and achieved a high quality score. This is why Michelin Stars are so coveted.

Action

This is one of the most crucial aspects of your advertisement. If all the other phases go well and there is no action, then you have failed. You must say exactly what you want readers to do. 'Call now,' or 'Visit our website now' are the final triggers that enable prospects to take action on an offer that they have been stimulated by.

It can sometimes help to introduce an element of scarcity. 'First come, first served,' or 'Free to the first 50 callers,' can be very powerful incentives. It is particularly useful in special offers that are available for a limited period: 'Special lunch price only available until 30 April.'

◆ **TIP** ◆

If any offers are available on the internet, make sure that you update the details and withdraw the offer when you say you will. How many sites do you look at where the Easter offers are still shown in the summer?

If you offer a phone number, make sure that it is answered efficiently. For an impulse buy, the phone is the preferred option. If you expect a large number of calls you should consider making an agreement with an answering service.

Advertorial

We are all assaulted with thousands of media messages each day. There is huge competition for a share of consumers' attention.

It seems that there is a greater degree of scepticism about advertising. However there is some benefit in producing your advertisement as an 'advertorial'. This is still an advertisement, but the layout is in the style of the magazine. The benefit is that it looks more credible, because of the editorial emphasis. It is also more of a soft sell. The only drawback is that it is more difficult to incorporate a good 'call to action', but you can ask the publication for reprints and use them in your mailings and sales calls.

Measuring effectiveness

No independent accommodation business has money to waste on ineffective advertising. You want to know that your objectives have been achieved. At the very least you need to know:

- the number of responses;
- how many responses were converted to a sale;
- how much that was worth.

Balance these results against the cost of the advertisement and you can make your mind up about the profitability of the campaign.

If you have the facilities, it is good to have separate incoming phone lines for different promotions. If you are directing visitors to your website, then set up specific landing pages for each promotion.

Often this accountability goes wrong at reception when they forget to ask enquirers the right question. The whole team needs to be part of the promotion plan so that they understand that advertising is an investment in everyone's success.

What to pay

The costs of advertising space can make your eyes water. But if you are clever you can negotiate some better deals. Firstly, it is important that the advertising sales executive you talk to understands that you are only having the conversation based on the understanding that you need a better rate: this usually gets the relationship off on the correct foot and may elicit a good offer.

Secondly only book your advertisement near to the deadline. This can backfire if you have a time-limited offer but can work to your advantage. Whatever you do, don't place an advert just because you get a last-minute offer.

In newspapers and magazines your eyes are automatically drawn to the right hand page. Always ask for a guarantee of this position before you sign any contract.

If you are talking to radio stations it can be worth discussing the idea of bartering. Stations can often use your facilities for prizes or for accommodation for their executives.

Internet advertising

Pay-per-click (PPC) advertising is probably the biggest revolution that has affected the hotel industry in the last 30 years. A big claim maybe, but understandable. The biggest advertising problem for independent hotels has always been the total cost of media space relative to the benefit. It costs a small ten-room hotel the same to advertise as it does a franchise with 500 hotels.

Now, with pay-per-click, you can just pay for the positive responses to your message, stop advertising when you have sold your inventory, and set a limit on your total advertising costs. Nirvana!

◆ TIP ◆

You still need a website that sells; attracting visitors is one thing, getting them to buy is another. Also, because it is so effective the individual costs per click can be considerable. But so long as you test and measure your effort, you can predict your costs of acquiring room nights.

Pay-per-click was first introduced by Overture but the first search engine to make PPC really easy to use was Google with their Adwords. Now the other main search engines MSN (MSN AdCenter) and Yahoo! (Yahoo Search Marketing Solutions) have developed their own systems. All of them are a little different but through the systems you can get help with choosing keywords to advertise with.

Although the advent of PPC has been a boon for small advertisers there is a small problem of click fraud. Your competitors (or anyone else for that matter) can easily sit at their computer and just click away on your ad. You have to pay for the clicks, your budget gets used up and your advert disappears until the next month. The search engines will always be on the look out for this type of activity and you need to communicate with them if you feel that this is happening to you.

Another drawback of pay-per-click is that people have to be specifically looking for your service. A new development is the possibility to actually just advertise on sites where you think your prospects might be searching, but for something else. This is called CPM, or cost per thousand impressions, and you pay every time your ad is seen on these other websites.

This AdSense facility is available on Google and although the costs are low, your ad could be seen by thousands of people (depending on the popularity of the site), so you have to keep an eye on your account and set your daily budget low, otherwise the media owner will rapidly evacuate your bank account. Whatever you do, don't advertise this way unless you are convinced that your own site is really set up to sell whenever you get the click throughs.

KEY POINTS

- Independent hotels should probably avoid image advertising, although this can work in the launch phase.

- Advertising works best if you have a long-term plan and stick to it.

- If publications contact you with 'great deals' the answer should be 'no'.

- If you can't measure the results of an advertisement then cancel it. That is after you have checked carefully what result the ad was constructed to deliver.

- Internet advertising can deliver good traffic to your internet site but it will only work if your site is optimised to sell.

7

Media Relations

Free publicity is just what you want, but nothing is ever really 'free'. It takes a lot of planning and effort to develop good relations with the media. But it can definitely be a profitable investment.

WORTH THE EFFORT

Being featured in your local, or even national, media can be one of the most cost-effective ways to promote a hospitality business. Hotels and restaurants are intrinsically interesting to a wide range of consumers and generally have a high profile in the local community. A sustained effort with the media can help you create word-of-mouth recommendations and a clear personality. Good local relationships can also be helpful should you ever need help to combat some local publicity that might not be to your advantage. No, any publicity is not good publicity!

> The major benefit is that whatever is said about you is seen as an endorsement. It is not you talking about your service (people often distrust an advertisement) but someone else giving it coverage as part of story.

As with any project, it takes time and effort to generate the circumstances under which you can create free publicity. This publicity can be extremely helpful when combined with your other efforts (direct contact and direct marketing) to generate extra revenue for your business.

The main difficulty is measuring the results of your efforts. If you do everything yourself then you only incur the opportunity cost of all the time spent with journalists. Traditionally results are measured in the number of column inches in media. This is a very subjective way of doing it and does not really prove the impact on your bottom line. Particularly if working with an agency, it is far better to set some specific objectives and then see whether they are achieved or not. Good Public Relations (PR) (although here we are only dealing with media relations) works well in combination with your other sales and promotional activities (a new launch for example) where you can then measure the total outcome from the total input of costs and effort.

Speak to any journalist and they will tell you how many hundreds of press releases come into their organisation. The majority are boring and hardly get read. Make sure that yours are in the top three per cent that make it.

What do journalists need?

Journalists need to fill their papers, magazines, radio and TV with interesting information. This is the bottom line. If you can help them with their task then you are guaranteed coverage of your hotel.

The media is a business just like the one you are in. They are in competition with each other, they have targets and they are evaluated to see if they have been successful. Come up with something that is quirky or creative and you will be at the front of the queue.

How to meet those needs

You can meet the needs of journalists by giving them what they want. This depends on the media that they are employed by. You have to make sure that the business editor only gets business news and that the women's magazines only get news related to women's issues.

You have to deliver them the information in the way that they want it: some will want e-mails and some faxes.

- **Newspapers and magazines** want items that are interesting, informative and educational.

- **Radio** works better with news that is a bit more unusual or off the wall.

- **TV** needs anything that looks interesting and is newsworthy from the viewers' point of view.

How to pitch

Editors and journalists are busy people, particularly around deadline (usually from 2pm onwards for daily morning papers) so check to make sure you avoid this stressful time. Nevertheless the lifeblood of any publication is information; they really do need your relevant story.

- Pitch in about 20 seconds with something newsworthy either on the phone personally or to voicemail. Check that they are ready for your pitch.

- Don't sound as if you are reading from a script.

- Make your story exciting and relevant to their needs.

- Include statistics if you can. Surveys sell.

- Follow up immediately if asked for more information.

- Maybe send a pitch letter first, rather than a press release.

- Try to involve the journalist prior to the event – maybe they can try out your new spa prior to the official launch?

Ideally the media will contact you before you contact them. This only happens if you can give an expert opinion that will help them write their copy for the looming deadline.

How to be newsworthy

There are any number of reasons to send a news release. Some arise as part of your business and some you can manufacture in order to gain free publicity. Use this list to prompt you to make your own annual plan.

- accomplishments
- anniversaries
- annual awards
- children's day
- contributions to charities
- customer surveys
- customer stories
- employee trips
- expanded facilities
- expert article
- first to offer a service
- free offer
- guest speaker
- historical tie in
- holiday events
- new employees
- open house
- personal story
- partnerships
- prediction
- reactions to breaking news
- research
- retirement
- sales promotions
- special events
- sponsorship
- trends
- visit by celebrity

The news release

Traditional media

Your news release needs to be reasonably short. Preferably on one page, about 250 words and double spaced. Make the paragraphs self-contained so that copy can be lifted straight into an article or used in its entirety. Write as you would like to see it in the publication but study their style in advance. Just state the facts and don't over-hype your service or achievements. Use adjectives very sparingly and remember who, where, why and when in the first paragraph.

Develop an enticing headline to grab attention, since journalists probably won't give you more than a few seconds to interest them. Try to avoid words like 'announce' or 'announcement'. They are overworked and date your information. Always put someone's contact details on the release and make sure that they are available to answer questions or give further details. Don't forget to date the release.

A photo is really what newspapers want. Not the typical 'grip and grin' style with two people shaking hands over a giant-sized cheque. They want something interesting, different and a bit quirky or unusual. Let your imagination run wild and then take the photo or get a professional in. It is far better to have a close up of two people than a shot of 20 where you can't see who is who.

Don't send these photos unless you are asked to. Mention that they are available in the press release and then wait to be asked for them. Alternatively publish them on your website and make them downloadable by the journalist.

Electronic media

Many people and organisations have signed up with Google News and Yahoo! News to receive online press releases based on certain keywords that they have submitted. Apparently, 27 million people use these news portals every month and a well-optimised press release can reach the first page of these news services within 24 hours. After this they can then find their way onto the regular search engine in less than a week and stay there for six months.

When you are creating an optimised press release you need to put your two primary keywords into the headline and the sub headline. Add a link to your site (or a specially constructed page on your site about what is in the release) and then submit the release to all the online wire services. Of course, just as in the offline world, you need to have something interesting to say and your release must be well written.

Press pack

Your press pack is to help a journalist get easy access to background material on your hotel. It is not for using as a direct mail piece. All details should be very factual, with few adjectives. You will need:

- **Background**: about your hotel, its history, facilities and contact details. Highlight what is unique and quantify your offer. Statistics help.

- **Biographies**: short profiles of the owner and chef plus anyone else with an interesting story (e.g. housekeeper been with hotel since it opened in 1969).

- **Photographs**: use a professional if possible and include pictures to go with the biographies plus illustrations of key facilities. Put them on CD for easy access.

Tips for dealing with journalists

- Don't hassle journalists after you have sent the release.
- Send to only one contact at each publication.
- Find out deadlines and send well in advance.
- Only send the release if contents are different and newsworthy.
- Always include your contact details.
- Don't send attachments to e-mails.
- Always check address and contact details.
- Let journalists/food writers eat alone in your restaurant if they wish.
- Always be available for further information request.
- Don't try to set terms for an interview.
- Make sure you have read the publication that you are sending a release to.

Guide books

There is a proliferation of guidebooks and over the years both their ownership and their editorial policy seems to have changed. But do your customers and guest still use them to guide them on where to eat or to stay? No one knows the answer, but I suspect that some of your prospects do take notice of these guides. Hopefully your local market will have no need to take any notice of whether you are in or out since you will have done such a good promotional job.

It is easy to get very upset if you are left out of a particular guide and your inferior colleague down the road is included. Remember, however, that any assessment is usually only on one occasion and maybe you had a bad day when the inspector called. My view is that an entry in a guide might be useful but it is probably not worth putting any real effort into being included. Be particularly wary of guides that ask you for payment for inclusion. The best guides are good enough to be supported by the readers. Your entry may lead to a marginal increase in covers or room nights but you shouldn't have any marketing plan that relies on there being any benefit. In other words, entries are the icing on the cake but your sales job is about making the cake in the first place.

Agency or DIY

There is a lot to be said for handing over the whole task to an agency. For a start they already have the contacts and they can hit the ground running. Fees, however, are often prohibitive for most independent hotels – monthly fees of around £1,500–2,000 are the norm. For most independent hotels this is not an option. More appropriate might be a project fee paid to a freelance PR consultant. Here fees are from £250 per day.

It really depends on how important PR is in your overall marketing mix and what sort of resources you are willing to allocate to do the job well. If you use all the techniques here you can do it yourself and see whether you benefit or not. You can then always go to an agency knowing exactly how it works.

Agency contract/expectation

If you do contract an agency you will need to set down the terms of business. These should cover:

- exclusivity
- contract term and cancellation
- fees
- billing procedures
- disbursements and expenses
- agency in-house costs
- payment terms
- approvals and authority
- copyright
- confidential information
- insurance
- applicable law.

The agency will also need to provide you with an outline of the agreed objectives and exactly what they are going to do to achieve these objectives:

- background
- objectives
- communication strategy
- key audiences

♦ messages
♦ implementation plan
♦ evaluation.

Measuring results

This is usually where most agency relationships founder and where you wonder whether it is worth the effort. A great public profile doesn't help if your hotel or restaurant is empty. Press clippings are not a great alternative to cash in the till.

Your media strategy needs to be part of your overall marketing plan, since if you just do PR the outcome is unlikely to be successful or the benefits sustained. Set your return on investment goals as realistically as possible and then be very strict about measuring whether or not these have been achieved. For instance, if you were launching a new restaurant, it would be reasonable to have a number of PR objectives such as:

1 Organise a launch party with 100 local 'movers and shakers'.

2 Generate 100 couples from the target market for two weeks of sample tastings.

3 Have three write ups in local media within two months.

All these objectives can be easily measured because you have specified those aspects that can be influenced by your agency or your own team if you have the resources.

KEY POINTS

♦ Exposure in the media is great but is usually the result of a lot of sustained effort.

- Journalists don't care about your business; they are in the business of publicising things that are of interest to their readers. Meet their needs and they will meet yours.

- Whatever your product, you can find an opportunity that will be of interest to a local or national audience. Brainstorm with your team and be creative.

- Don't neglect the electronic media potential.

- Even though it is difficult, you must somehow try to measure the results of your media efforts.

8

Promotional Materials and Activity

Most hotels have a very strong local market, which responds well to tactical sales promotion activity. Traditional activity works very well if it is planned properly but efforts to make your internet site effective will be well rewarded.

SALES PROMOTION

Sales promotion is a great way of counteracting competitor activity, converting prospects into customers or launching new facilities. Tactical mailing distributed door-to-door is an excellent way of promoting new restaurant openings, new menus or new facilities such as a leisure club.

The simplest promotions are price based. There are conflicting views on the wisdom of these. Consumers can be rather sceptical, particularly if you over use 'special prices'. When does a sale price become the normal price and then cease to have any value?

◆ TIP ◆

Customers for your hotel or restaurant are likely to use your competition, so price promotion just encourages them to shop around. Ideally you want customers to form an emotional bond with your service, so that any price promotion is rendered redundant.

Sales promotion techniques tend to be used more in the retail sector where there is an imperative to generate market share or launch new products in a crowded market. These promotions can be directed to the consumer, to sales staff, to retailers and to wholesalers. They can involve:

◆ coupons
◆ discounts
◆ contests
◆ point of sale displays
◆ rebates
◆ gifts and incentives.

Hotels have not traditionally been seen as a service where consumers would normally expect a price promotion. However if you choose your media carefully your image will not be damaged. Some of the weekday lunch promotions in up-market daily newspapers are very effective at bringing in new customers to even the most prestigious hotel or restaurant. Most people are up for a deal, whoever they are or however much they earn. It is a moot point whether or not these sort of promotions build long-term customer relationships, although sales promotion is also an effective way of promoting the facilities you have to your current guests.

It is easy to fall into the trap of using very formal language whenever you promote events or facilities in-house. Don't lose your own tone of voice; for instance if you use a humorous style in your brochures then keep on using it.

Leaflets

If you do produce leaflets to promote any element of your business you need to take great care with the production. This is not to say that it needs to be particularly expensive, but it does need to be appropriate to the product that you are promoting. If you have a high quality restaurant with an expensive menu, then any promotional leaflet needs to be of good quality; a flimsy 80gsm production will not do.

Just as with advertising and direct mail, getting attention is the key to success. If you plan a door-to-door mailing then mixing your leaflet up with all the others in a generic mailing or inserting in free newspapers will not work. It would be difficult enough to grab attention if you handed a copy to each prospect individually, so the least you can do is drop the leaflet through each door on its own.

Writing copy for a leaflet is the same as writing for direct mail or advertising. You need to grab your readers' attention and make them interested enough to take whatever action you want. You also need some of the techniques of a poster, where you keep the copy to a minimum and just give enough information for the decision to be made.

Leaflets are associated with offers and offers are designed to attract new prospects. Always:

- Put the offer in the headline so it is seen immediately.
- Make the offer easy to understand.
- Make the offer specific.
- Say exactly what needs to be done to take up the offer.
- Add a special incentive for acting today.
- Give options for responding (phone, e-mail, fax etc).
- Put a deadline on the offer.

Banners

Banners can be really effective, but they can also be really awful. It is all in the execution. Some of those building wraps that you see in city centres are really impressive and convey a great image about the building project that is under construction. Banners work when they are very temporary and convey something that is time related. Often the information refers to a price promotion or an announcement of a new facility.

Viewers need to be surprised and intrigued enough to assimilate the few words that it is possible to put on any banner. As with any signage, the quality of the banner must be consistent with the image of your hotel. You can buy really cheap versions but you need to spend the right money to stay consistent with your image in the market. Make sure that you work out how to fix the banner before you order it and ensure that the scale of the banner fits the situation. Torn and broken banners that stay up for months really do not do you any favours.

If you have an interesting calendar of events in your restaurant then a series of banners can be effective, so long as you distinguish one from the other and make sure that the right announcement goes up at the right time. But the big proviso is that banners are only cost-effective if you have a good level of passing traffic, either on foot or by car.

A-boards

Generally A-boards are used because you cannot get permission for a more permanent sign. Often you are placing them on public property and the local authority will try and have them removed. It's all a bit of a game but as long as you stick to the 'rules' these boards can be a useful part of your sales promotion. They are great for price promotions, such as special lunch or dinner menus. Again the quality of the board is key. If they are broken/faded or badly written they do you no favours, conveying a couldn't care less attitude to your service.

Be careful about using the whole rainbow of colour options on chalkboards. Find or train someone to write the sign well or contact a specialist signwriter.

Use as few words as you can, since passers-by only have a few seconds to take in the information. I like the boards that have a panel on them that you can change, so you can promote, for example, morning coffee, lunch and afternoon tea in succession. Of course it then becomes an operational issue to ensure that the right promotion is showing at the right time.

Posters

Posters are a great way to promote your in-house facilities. You may also have the opportunity to display a poster promoting an element of your business at a remote location, say in a shop or at a reservation office. Use as few words as possible, so long as you get the message across. Start at the top (where people start reading) with something to grab attention (not your hotel name, which probably need not be included at all if it is a poster designed to be put up in the hotel itself!).

Don't promote features: use a benefit instead but keep it short. A poster has to be readable in about three seconds, so hone the copy and delete any words that don't work very hard. Analyse each word and see if it can be left out. Pictures work well, but ensure the words and the pictures deliver the same message. Look for positions where people are not occupied doing something else. Put the poster at eye level and make sure it is well lit. If there is a place where guests have to wait (say at an elevator) use some spare space for a poster.

In-house promotion

It is dangerous to assume that every visitor to your hotel, whether as a guest or restaurant customer, knows everything that you offer. If you are primarily a pub or restaurant with rooms, ask ten customers about your bedrooms: it is unlikely that all ten will know that you have them. Do all your guests know that you serve afternoon tea between three and five pm?

I would not advocate that you produce a piece of promotional material for every service you provide. Very soon a bedroom can look like a paper store, with lots of scruffy tent cards cluttering the writing area. However, if you don't tell people what services you provide, how will they ever take advantage of them?

> Ensure that any promotional piece conforms to all the right rules about copywriting. Assume that a tent card is a poster. Keep it bright, visual, interesting, make a strong proposition and invite some action.

In-room guest information can also be used effectively. Try to sell the benefits and remove all those negatives that creep into the instructions. For example, turn 'We don't accept etc...' into 'We are delighted to accept...'. Why not create guest information that is tailored to your different guest segments? Weekday business travellers need different information from weekend leisure guests. Maybe you can print out something bespoke and hand it to each guest on arrival along with a welcome drink. This way you can also take into account guests from other countries and produce information in their language.

Legal checklist

Sales promotions can be a minefield of regulation. There is a long list of things that you can and can't do. If you are using an agency then this is not too much of a problem since they should check that you are legal. If you do it yourself, consider that there are more than likely to be rules covering any promotion that involves the following:

- alcohol
- bank notes
- children
- competitions
- coupons
- data protection
- disability

- lotteries
- mailing preference
- mock auctions
- prices
- racial discrimination
- service marks
- testimonials

- ◆ free draws
- ◆ identity of promoter
- ◆ instant wins

- ◆ trade description
- ◆ trademarks.

BROCHURES

The subject of brochures is fascinating. I have seen hotels with no brochure, hotels with brochures that they are reluctant to give away because of the cost, and hotels with brochures that give the completely wrong impression of the product and its service.

The most important factor is not to start your sales planning with the brochure: it is only a tool and you cannot select the tool until you have decided what job needs doing. There is nothing more frustrating than producing 5,000 brochures and then wondering what to do with them.

This is why I wouldn't go so far as to say that every hotel definitely needs a brochure to be successful. Sometimes hotels produce expensive brochures and think that they will be successful just by doing a mailing or leaving a pile in reception. Nevertheless, an appropriate brochure that leaves the correct impression with the recipient, combined with a well-thought out distribution strategy, can be very useful.

◆ **TIP** ◆

Think through your strategy first and then decide if a brochure would be helpful. If you are a small hotel, and all your business comes from local businesses through your personal sales effort, you should question the need for a brochure at all.

Generally, specialisation is the key. Catch-all brochures that are aimed at weekend visitors, meeting planners and corporate guests generally miss the target. Prospective guests looking for a romantic weekend might well be put off if they see that you specialise in corporate meetings. Look at your facilities and think through what sort of leaflet or brochure you need for the promotion of each segment:

- weekend/leisure guests
- corporate stayers
- wedding guests
- conference (meetings/team building etc)
- leisure membership
- spa.

Certainly, if you have conference facilities or cater specifically for weddings then you do need some comprehensive printed literature. Whatever you do, make sure this literature isn't a straightjacket for the prospect. Everybody wants to be thought of as an individual, so the sales letter is the important piece, with the literature as a back up.

I would never, ever recommend leaving conference or wedding packs at reception so that weekend staff can give them to prospects. Every brochure fulfilment must be tailor made, and do make sure that staff are trained to collect enough information for effective follow up on the Monday.

Style and format
The subject of style is almost the same as cost. You will never be

sure who gets hold of your brochures and you must work on the theory that the more that you give away the better. Taking this into account, how much do you want to spend? It is very nice having a stylish brochure in an unusual shape with each page separated by tissue paper; but if each copy costs around £5 how many copies will you be happy to give away?

First check the competition and see what they do. Then do something different! A well-produced DL leaflet ($^1/_3$ A4) can work really well and because of its low cost (around six pence each) you can give away heaps.

Wedding and meeting information is slightly different, since you know who is getting the material. You won't send this information as a direct mail piece before you know exactly what your prospects' needs are. Thus cost is less important since the cost of, say, £4 per copy is not so great compared with the wedding or meeting that could be worth up to £5,000. Developing comprehensive and useful material takes time, but remember that a client will be evaluating a number of offers together so you need to stand out from the crowd.

This does not mean you have to spend more on the literature or produce a weightier volume. You will stand out if you:

- are less conventional in your thinking;
- think about everything from the customers' point of view;
- concentrate on benefits not features;
- customise the information for each market segment.

Copywriting

Your brochure should follow most of the rules that have already been covered in Chapters 5 and 6. Look at most hotel brochures and you will find that they follow very few of them.

- Grab attention with headings and headlines.

- Make sure you concentrate the copy on benefits to the customer.

- Try to get across your philosophy and your vision.

- Don't fill every available space with words or pictures; leave some white space.

- Keep sentences and words short and write as you would talk.

- Use bullets for easy readability.

- Include quotes from satisfied guests but ask their permission first.

- Show the copy draft to a stranger, or at least someone unconnected to you.

- Don't include any information that is likely to change, such as room rates.

- Check all spellings, particularly of place names, and contact details.

With brochures that are aimed at weekend visitors or corporate users the copy is not as important as the visual impression, and should be kept to a minimum. The colour, design, photographs and paper should all combine to give the correct impression of your hotel. It is very nice to have a 12-page brochure with tissue paper interleaves but can you, or do you want to, live up to the expectation that this produces?

Be careful about making exaggerated claims. Holiday brochures that cleverly omit any mention of the road that separates the hotel from the beach have caught many of us out. Ensure that you can substantiate each of your claims. You may think that one exercise bike is plenty for you but you can't really describe it as a gymnasium.

Photography

Photographic style is subject to fashion and there has definitely been a move a way from staged photos that portray the whole bedroom or restaurant. Not that I would endorse promoting style over substance but the images that work well are exactly that – an image.

◆ TIP ◆

There is no need to hire models and set up elaborate photo sessions, unless you are making reference photos for conference buyers. It is far more effective to find features of your building and services that give an accurate representation of the sort of service that a prospective customer can expect.

If you commission a professional photographer you have to consider the issue of copyright. Copyright on the images actually belongs to the photographer but you will have an implied licence to use them for the purpose they were commissioned, such as a brochure. If you need to use the images for other purposes such as for postcards or your internet site as well, you will need to obtain an assignment. This needs to be in writing and signed by the photographer.

Production

It is possible to do everything yourself including arranging the printing of brochures. This though is probably not the best use of your time. Design or marketing agencies are likely to be able to negotiate more favourable prices, which can compensate for the cost of their input.

YOUR INTERNET SITE

The internet is becoming more and more vital to the distribution of your hotel rooms. It is said that around 25–35 per cent of any hotel's reservations originate from a guest's interaction with the internet. It is more and more important to get your total internet strategy working for you. Although changing all the time, it is generally agreed that up to 75 per cent of travellers now use search engines before making a booking, with most using broad generic search terms. A successful internet strategy will address two major issues:

♦ Your site needs to be optimised so that the spiders sent out by the search engines pick it up and feature it in the organic search listing. (Google provides guidelines on how to build a 'crawler-friendly' site at www.google.com/webmasters/guidelines.html.)

♦ Your site needs to give each visitor a rewarding experience. This is particularly vital if you decide to advertise your site through pay-per-click (PPC) or pay per thousand impressions (PPM) – that way you will generate the response you want.

The internet has also given independent hotels the biggest boost for decades. Now that internet distribution systems are becoming better understood and there is more transparency, it is possible for independents to use third party sites and their distribution muscle to combat the branded operations. Many independents are now receiving up to 35 per cent of their total sales online, just like their franchise competition. However you have to be careful. There are many traps waiting for the unwary, particularly from agencies charging high commissions and demands for lowest rate guarantees.

The advent of PPC and PPM advertising has also levelled the playing field between the chains and the independents.

Do you need a site? I don't think that there is any need for much discussion on this subject. If you have rooms to sell then you need a website. The only discussion is what sort and how much to spend on it. You also need to offer an online booking capability.

Fortunately most of the techniques for making a success of a website are the same techniques as those that make direct mail so successful.

- Decide exactly what you are trying to achieve with your site.
- Grab people's attention.
- Excite them enough to want to make a purchasing decision.

There really is nothing new under the sun.

Techniques for building a great website

After spending a great deal of money to build their web presence, the majority of accommodation businesses coming online are disappointed with the results from their website. It is quite likely that graphic designers and technical developers that have no real marketing experience built most of these under-performing websites.

Unfortunately people do just 'surf' the web and you often have no more than eight seconds to interest visitors enough to keep them from clicking off your home page. Even if they do stay, the average conversion of visitors to prospects is as low as one per cent; quite a challenge!

Having reviewed hundreds of hotel websites, I have seen the same mistakes being made over and over. As the internet develops and thousands of sites are added every month, users are becoming very 'site aware' and they get irritated with poor performing sites. No one has any patience any more. The most annoying featured are deemed to be:

- pop-up ads
- need for extra software to view site
- dead links
- confusing navigation
- registration to access contents
- slow-loading pages.

This section focuses mostly on the public face of your site rather than the technical aspects of the behind-the-scenes coding. This is also just as vital to get right. If you are interested your web designer will be able to explain the intricacies of HTML, CSS, JavaScript and meta information.

So that you can produce a top-of-the-range website, here are some techniques, in no particular order, that will ensure that you have a website that really performs for you.

Use a professional

It is relatively simple (so I am told!) to produce a basic website. There are good software packages (from FrontPage to XsitePro) that anyone with a bit of know-how can use (as a matter of interest, professionals tend to use Macromedia Dreamweaver but it is expensive; New-view at nvu.com may be a good alternative). And because of their ready availability there are plenty of offers from friends and contacts to put something together for you. Try to resist the temptation!

Developing a good site that sells is not that easy. You need technical skills as well as the ability to write text and graphically design something appropriate to your market. Not only this, you also need some marketing perspective to ensure that you are using all these techniques!

Use a professional who has developed sites that you like and that actually work. You don't need to spend a fortune and you can have a good site built for around £400. If you want your site to be more dynamic, with interactive features such as e-mail capture, then cost will be nearer £750.

Clearly differentiate your offer

How many websites have you been to that look the same and have the same functions? People go to your site to look for somewhere to stay or a place to eat. They want to know if your venue meets their needs.

All visitors to your site must have a clear understanding of why you are different and that you are the only solution for them to choose; if it is not clear they will move on to your competitor.

Your differences must benefit the customer. To find out what customers appreciate about your hotel just ask them why they use your hotel, or look at some of the compliment letters that you should have on file. Emphasise your positioning throughout your site.

Register appropriate domain

You should give your site the simplest but most appropriate name possible. The closest it is to what your customers call you the better. Hotels have an advantage, although, for instance, there are hundreds of Fairview Hotels, there are probably not that many in each location. So www.FairviewHotelLeeds.com is a reasonably logical and easy to remember address. You could also leave out 'Hotel'.

Some points to remember:

- Try to obtain the .com/.co.uk/ extension rather than .org or .info.

- Don't use hyphens in the address. They are unexpected and confusing.

- The shorter the address the better, but not strange abbreviations.

Choosing your keywords

This is probably the most important thing you can do to ensure the success of your website. Why is this? Imagine a searcher visiting one of the major search engines; he types in a topic word and up come the results, ten per page. If he knows you, then using the name of your hotel might get you into the top ten, so long as there aren't that many hotels with the same name. But the key to successful searching is making sure that what you offer fits in with what the visitor wants.

To find the best keywords and phrases for your business, ask your customers, or someone outside your business, what they would type in the search engine's search window when looking for your site.

Optimise each page separately

You must consider the focus of each page separately. Create content-rich pages that concentrate on one or two topics only. For instance, make separate pages for Location, Meetings, Accommodation and Restaurant etc and then try to drive traffic to each page by having different keywords or phrases for each (no more than five each).

If you want to see how other hotels do it, call up their site, click on your 'View' toolbar and then open 'Source' and look at their keyword meta tag use. Their site may not be working that well but it might help you!

Consider your offer

Obviously, the more specific you can be the better. Using just the word 'hotel' is no good since there are hundreds of thousands of hotels. Add specific location indicators such as 'Edinburgh' plus some speciality such as 'no smoking' or 'boutique' etc to make up multiple word key phrases such as 'meetings Edinburgh'.

Help with keywords

You can subscribe to a site like www.wordtracker.com for help with finding keywords that people are actually searching for. Use their keyword effectiveness index (KEI) to see what the competition is for specific keywords. There is also a free option on http://.inventory.overture.com and you can use the Google tool at http://adwords.google.co.uk/select/

Where to put them

When a search engine visits your site it look at the source code of your site (in HTML) not the fancy design. It considers anything that's towards the top of the page to be more relevant. Therefore the <head> section of your web page is extremely important. Unfortunately all search engines treat Meta tags differently (in fact Google no longer uses the meta description tag). Nevertheless the most important meta tags are the 'title' (no more than 60 characters), 'description' and 'keywords' (fewer than 30 words each), since one or other of them is used by most search engines.

◆ TIP ◆

Remember to place your keywords or phrases early on in the body text. Some search engines retrieve the first few lines of your web page and utilise them as the description of your site in the search results, so make sure they stand up alone and describe you as you wish. Make the first 25 words of your copy keyword rich. Sometimes the keywords in bold can help.

Relevance

Whatever you do, if you put a keyword in the source code, do make sure that it is used in the text for that page. Don't overdo it or you will be blacklisted for spamming; at least twice will do. In other words, don't try to outsmart the search engines just because they are computer systems. At some stage they will catch on. Be honest and straightforward and if your site is interesting and the codes are relevant to searchers, you should gain prominence in the rankings.

Update your site regularly

You can make a very static site with no information in it that changes. However this does not take real advantage of the power of the internet. Also, the search engine spiders will see that your site has not been updated for a while and give it less prominence. You need to generate traffic that comes back often and customers that take some action as a result of their visit.

There are many opportunities to include lots of changing information:

- special offers
- calendar of events
- download vouchers
- last-minute rates.

Capture e-mail addresses

Perhaps one of the biggest mistakes is failing to proactively capture your visitors' names and e-mail addresses. This is critical because, once you have them, you can use them again and again free of charge.

As your visitors roam your site they may be impressed enough with your content to sign up to your newsletter or download a voucher. By placing your opt-in box (a form that captures your visitor's e-mail address) on every web page, you'll continually remind your visitor to give you their name and e-mail address. Think of different offers to make on each page, but keep them relevant to the page subject. For example on the Meetings page give a guarantee voucher or an opportunity to upgrade a coffee break.

The industry average sign-up rate is around five per cent. If your sign-up rate is below five per cent you need to provide something of stronger value to encourage your visitor. They need a really strong reason to share their personal contact information with you.

Use compelling headlines

It is said that 80 per cent of the success of a direct mail letter is attributed to its headline. It is no different with website copy. The web has brought universal access to photos and graphics, but in the end it's the copy that sells. The trick to getting your visitors to read your copy is to use dynamic, attention-getting headlines and sub-headlines.

◆ **TIP** ◆

The sole purpose of your headline should be to make your visitor want to continue reading the text below it. Every page of your website should start with a headline. You may even want to use a sub-headline to support your main headline.

Throughout your copy you should continue to use sub-headlines as a way to break up your copy and to allow your visitor to 'skim' your content. Most web surfers just skim the text, so the chances of having your copy read without the use of sub-headlines are slim. People are eight times more likely to read your content if you have a headline.

Exciting content

Many web developers don't seem to know how to write web copy, which explains why most hotel sites have text that is boring and predictable. Make sure that pages are not cluttered and that everything is clear straight away. Content is more important than pictures.

The most important piece of information is the opening paragraph of the home page. It must be short, succinct and to the point. When writing copy for websites you need to use a newspaper copy technique: put the conclusion first and follow with when, what, where and how. Don't be tempted to write a conventional story with a beginning, middle and conclusion.

You can also put keywords in the name of the page, e.g. www.yoursite.com/meetings_london.htm. Make sure that the phrase is broken up like this so that the search engine spiders will see them as individual words in a phrase.

Below are some ideas on how to make your text a bit more interesting.

Use case studies

Case studies are a useful way to demonstrate your credibility by proving your ability to get results. They also give the reader a glimpse of the benefits they can expect to achieve if they use your hotel. They answer the 'What's in it for me?' question. This is particularly relevant to meeting room facilities. When you present case studies, use the Problem-Solution-Results format.

Use short words and paragraphs

To make your copy easy to read, use short words and paragraphs. There is nothing more uninviting than a 20-line paragraph that looks like a sea of words. People won't read it, no matter how interesting it really is.

Break the text into smaller paragraphs with no more then five lines each, and include sub-headings to introduce new topics. Remember that it takes about 20 per cent longer to read something on a computer screen than it does on paper.

Be careful about the font you use and do check and double-check all spellings and grammar. Having got visitors to your site the last thing you want to do is put them off with poor attention to detail.

Use clear navigation

If a visitor lands on your site and gets confused, they are only a short click away from another site. They are very unforgiving and will not waste time navigating a maze. You must provide good navigation of your website if you want to convert your visitors into customers. It is vital that you put most of your effort into making your site user-friendly. A good site map will also help the search engine spiders to navigate your site.

Here are a few ideas on developing good navigation:

Determine the response you want

The reason your website exists is to get response: this might be subscribing to your newsletter or making a reservation. Whatever it is, you need to decide what it is and develop a pathway.

Provide a pathway to your response

Providing a pathway means strategically designing your site to lead your visitors down a specific path that gets them to act. The easiest way to do this is to ask yourself, 'What is the *first* thing I want my visitor to do when they land on my site?'

Once you've decided that, it becomes much easier to design a site that starts your visitors off on their pathway. At each turning point in the pathway you need to ask yourself the same question, 'What is it that I want my visitor to do now?' Then design your site to help your visitor accomplish that thing first.

Provide a 'closing' page

When you are actually selling anything through your site your closing page should provide an irresistible offer that even you couldn't pass up. Make sure to remind your visitor of the benefits they'll receive, the relatively small risk that they're taking and why they need to act right now.

Navigational tips
- Use the top and left side of the web page for navigation.
- Always allow for a way to get back home.
- Place benefit statements on your navigation buttons.

Use graphics wisely

Many web developers can't resist using all their technical knowledge on your site. Resist at all costs. Check out all the sites that sell on the internet and you will see that, by and large, they are very simple.

Simplicity and clarity are the watchwords. Don't use frames and if you really do want to use flash, only do it on part of your site. The search engine spiders really don't like them. The use of blinking graphics can have its place if you want to emphasise a special offer or point something out.

Using overwhelming photos can also be distracting. In fact photos in general are a bit of a distraction both to the 'spiders' and the visitor. They should be used to complement the text not vice-versa.

Reinforce credibility

The average consumer (and corporate buyer) has learnt to be highly sceptical of anyone selling anything. On the internet, scepticism is even higher. Your biggest hurdle to making an online sale will be overcoming your customer's scepticism.

The following points will increase your credibility and instil a sense of trust and believability with your prospects.

Provide full contact information

On each of your web pages put your full contact information, including phone number. Make it as easy as possible for people to contact you, since that is really your main objective anyway. Be careful of putting your e-mail address – avoid having your address 'harvested' with the resultant spam potential. Using a form for people to contact you avoids this.

Include testimonials

There is nothing more persuasive than being recommended to stay somewhere, even if you don't know the people concerned. But if you do include testimonials, you must put the person's name and location plus a photograph if possible. An anonymous reference just will not do. You might have made it up yourself!

You can extract testimonials from letters sent in to you but always check with the sender that they are happy for you to use their details. Far more effective is to contact past guests soon after they leave or as they leave and ask them a series of questions related to your facilities and your positioning.

◆ TIP ◆

Be up front about wanting to use good comments to generate extra business. Your customers will probably be flattered.

Provide a guarantee

Providing a strong guarantee tells your visitor that you stand behind your product and that there is little risk in staying with you. It will overcome any initial reluctance to use your hotel since they have nothing to lose. If you have a meeting or conference product this is particularly useful in getting clients to try you for the first time.

There is often a fear that you will be taken advantage of and that guests will say they were unsatisfied just to get their money back. I think this is unfounded but if it does happen, think of all the extra customers you have gained.

Provide a picture of you and your staff
People don't buy from businesses and businesses don't buy from businesses. People buy from people, and people who work for businesses buy from people who work for businesses. The more you can include about you and your credentials and successes, the more people will feel good about doing business with you.

Focus content on your visitor

As in any situation where you are trying to 'sell' a service, you must ask yourself what it is the visitor is looking for that will benefit them. Consumers are self-centred and are looking for you to solve a particular problem, even if it is just what to buy their partner for his or her birthday. Think about everything from the visitors' point of view and encourage actions from their standpoint.

For instance, the page title could be 'Fairview Hotel – book rooms online'. No one is interested in how good you think you are or how many awards you have won (you might use this information if you are trying to reinforce credibility and can use it as third party endorsement).

If you've been in business for any period of time you've probably heard all the objections you get when you are selling your service. Make sure that you address all these in your text. Additionally you can cover them in a FAQ (frequently asked questions) section.

You will also be aware of the benefits of your hotel that sell best. Highlight these and go back over your copy to ensure that you have used benefits rather than features. At the same time make sure that you rewrite 'you' or 'your' wherever you have used 'I' or 'we'. Provide as much useful information as you can, particularly maps and local attractions.

◆ TIP ◆

Banners and pop-ups can distract a visitor and prevent them from acting on your desired response. Pop-ups are unpopular with search engines, and with visitors (although a case can be made for exit pop-ups to try to persuade someone to sign up for your newsletter when they initially decline).

Links

Your website developer must make sure that links will automatically open a second window with the destination site in it, but leave your site up and running. This way you will be able to achieve both goals. Avoid links from any pages that are sales related. Ensure that there are no broken links within your site or to external sites. You can obtain free software to check your links.

You can boost your site's popularity by the number and quality of links pointing to it. These links must be relevant to your offer so should come from local attractions, guidebooks, award organisations and tourism or local business associations. Find all the sites that you want links from, put a link to their site and then e-mail them to ask if they will provide a link to you. To find who links to your competition just enter 'link' followed by your competitor's domain in your favourite search engine.

Ensure your site loads quickly

Your site needs to load in fewer than ten seconds. If it takes any longer your potential guest will get very impatient and may well give up. Resist the temptation to place a lot of graphics that slow down your site.

- Build your page with the slowest user in mind.

- Build your web page no bigger that 50K including graphics. Your home page should be even less.

- Always use a compression tool to optimise graphics before you use them.

- Make sure your pictures load little by little so that a visitor can see that something is happening, even if slowly.

- Preload the images on your site. As your visitor reads your headline and opening copy, your other graphics will be loading in the background.

Track all visitors

It is vital that you are able to make changes to your site if it is not working to your satisfaction. It is a big investment and it needs to really work for you to get a return on your investment. The only way that you can see what is happening is to take measurements and evaluate the outcomes. Your web developer will be able to sign you up with a good service.

These are amongst the measurements that you should ask for:

Conversion rate

Taking the number of visitors to your site, and dividing it by the number that actually made a reservation, gives your conversion rate. Example: if one hundred people go to your site and five make a reservation, your sell-through is five per cent.

Visitor value

This measures how much each unique visitor that comes to your site is worth to you. For example, if five out of one hundred people make a reservation, and your sale value is £100, each visitor is worth £5 because 100 visitors equals £500 in sales.

Opt-in sign-up rate

Your opt-in rate is the percentage of people that sign up (give you their e-mail address) when they visit your site. For example, if 100 people visit your site and five give you permission to send them information by giving you their e-mail address, your opt-in rate is five per cent.

Visitor statistics

Sometimes visitors arrive at your site and leave from the home page. Over time you will be able to check this 'bounce' rate where you compare visitors who stay with visitors who leave straightaway. Also knowing how many first-time visitors come to your site daily is an important metric.

Source of visitors

Knowing where your traffic comes from is also important, especially if they are driven to your site through a paid promotion. Your web statistics package should be able to tell you which search engines your visitor originated from, in addition to the URLs of the websites your visitors came from.

Average visitor time

Knowing how much time your visitor spent on a certain web page (such as your home page) will let you know to what degree your visitor finds your site interesting. It can also tell you approximately where your visitors are jumping off. This metric is important to know for each web page.

Most viewed web pages

Knowing which of your web pages are popular and which ones aren't will tell you where your visitors' interests lie, how well your visitors stay on their pathway to the closing page, and what web pages should be dropped (or tweaked).

With all these metrics you'll be able to answer several key questions about your site's performance. But perhaps the most important is, 'How much is each unique visitor worth to me?' This key metric will drive all your decisions about how much you can spend to acquire new customers profitably. For example, if your visitor value is £1, you can't afford to pay £1.20 per click to drive new visitors to your site (unless you're strategically acquiring new customers at a loss).

How not to be banned

You will probably have read about all sorts of clever techniques that you can use to improve your site rankings on the search engines (Google, Yahoo and MSN being the most popular ones). As I have tried to emphasise in this section, the only really effective method is to create a site that appeals to your audience, provides quality content and contains meta information that is faithful to your site content.

The various search engines set up their search algorithms differently and no one can ever keep up to date with how they decide how to rank websites in their organic searches. It is really best not to worry about how to outwit a search engine. Even if you get one step ahead they employ some very clever people and will soon catch up.

To summarise some of the danger areas, you should avoid the following:

- **Excessive links**: Most importance is placed on quality appropriate links inbound to your site from a wide variety of sites, but don't acquire them too quickly. Outbound links are less important. Avoid anything to do with link farms that exist solely to trade in irrelevant links.

- **Cloaking**: This involves creating one page designed specifically for the search engines and another that will appear to the user.

- **Doorway pages**: Doorway or gateway pages are crammed full of keywords and are designed solely to get higher rankings. Your site will be penalised if you use these.

- **Cross-linking:** This is where you create multiple sites often with similar, or even identical, content. These are then linked together to increase your PageRank. This is not to say that if you have more than one site you cannot inter-link them.

- **Submitting multiple URLs from the same site:** If the search engines do not find your site, just submit your index page once. Don't submit more than one page from the same site.

- **Search engine software:** Don't use software that sends automatic submissions or queries to the search engines.

- **Pages loaded with irrelevant keywords:** Relevance is the key. If the keywords are in your text then you can put them in the code.

- **Hidden text or links:** Only use text or links that are visible to visitors.

KEY POINTS

- Regularly check the performance of your own site by typing your top keywords and key phrases into the search engines to see if you appear in the top five.

- Tags, links and properly written text are the key components of a website.

- Usability is the overriding consideration.

- Never forget that hotels are sold on the basics of location, facilities and things to do and see. But you must promote the benefits, not just the features.

- Keep it simple, appropriate and clear and you cannot go wrong.

- If you neglect your site so will the search engines; you must update regularly.

- Don't try to outwit the search engines.

- Don't expect miracles. It can take months to be found by the search engines so it is vital to be persistent.

- Once you have your site, make sure that you do everything you can both on- and off-line to direct visitors to it.

Part Three
Getting Where You Want To Be

Chapter 9 How Do You Price To Maximise Revenue?
Pricing challenges
Yield management

Chapter 10 How Do You Make Systems and Data Work For You?
How to measure customer satisfaction
Useful data to keep
Implement systems for an easier life

Chapter 11 What Tactics Can You Use To Develop Revenue?
Customer evaluation
Increasing revenue

Chapter 12 Planning Your Marketing Activity
What is left to do
Marketing plan format

'I have more respect for the fellow with a single idea who gets there, than the fellow with a thousand ideas who does nothing.'

Thomas Edison

9

How Do You Price
To Maximise Revenue?

Pricing correctly for each target market is vital but never use price alone as the reason to persuade prospects to use your hotel.

PRICING CHALLENGES

Your pricing policy is one of the major influences on your profitability. Set your prices too high and prospects will think that you are too expensive for the benefits offered; too low and customers may think that there is something wrong.

In an ideal world you would take your costs of doing business, estimate your likely occupancy and then work out an acceptable room rate. If you did this exercise I suspect that your room rates would be at least 30 per cent higher than your closest competition. During your investigation of your competition you will have established where you fit and what your headline rates should be. Hopefully if you combine the tactics in the previous section with some of the techniques in this section you will find some opportunities to close the gap, so that you actually do make some money.

The internet has had a big influence on hotel pricing, mostly due to the universal availability of your prices. There are no secrets anymore, so every decision you make must be consistent and, most of all, to your long-term advantage. However there are a great number of opportunities for the independent hotel to level the playing field with their chain compatriots. Here we will look at some areas where your policies need to be certain.

Pricing psychology

There are many well-known metrics that companies take into account before arriving at pricing decisions. Many of them apply to manufacturers and to retailers of goods. Hotel services are very different, in the same way that airlines and car hire companies have sales opportunities that are lost if not consumed immediately.

You are in a business where you cannot just take your costs of production and add a margin. You have limited supply and must maximise your opportunities when they present themselves. Here are some factors relevant to the hospitality business that you should take into account when setting your rates and prices.

Reference pricing

This is where your customer has a general expectation of a price level that seems reasonable and fair. Now the difficulty here is that you have no control over where they get their information to develop their expectations. In some ways this is to the benefit of the chains, since if your prospect knows the Hyatt in Birmingham, then they will have a good idea of the price of a Hyatt in any other location. When assessing your value for money, customers look at current and past price influences and the price of similar hotels.

At its most basic, if you have been quoted £100 online, made a booking and turn up outside what looks like a flea pit, you will feel inclined to get straight back in the taxi. On the other hand, if a concierge welcomes you and the hotel looks like a five star property you will congratulate yourself on securing a bargain.

Relative prices

It is not the actual price of your hotel that is important. More influential is the perception of a price difference, either since last time a similar purchase was made or against a competitor. This serves to emphasise the importance of surveying the competition and being realistic of the price differences that are justified by your service and facility differences.

Perceived value

No one would seriously contend that the hotel business is all about price. Mind you, by the behaviour of some companies you'd think that they had nothing else to offer! There is a huge range of hotel offerings, all at various prices. Guests pay £500 rather than £50 presumably because they feel that they get the value that they want.

The price that customers are prepared to pay is based on their perception of value. The whole of your marketing effort is directed at maximising this perception in the mind of your prospects. This is the basis of all brand advertising, where the intention is for you to perceive the value to be greater than its non-brand alternative, just because of the brand image.

Perceived value is usually described as a trade-off between quality and price. Your customer makes a perceived value judgement based on comparison of the actual benefits received with the actual sacrifices (price paid) endured. At the same time the customer compares the value received with the perceived value of other alternatives.

Unfortunately customers are often not in a good position to judge the true worth of a service, so you need to help them. You need to boost the perceived value by manipulating the customer's frame of reference.

◆ TIP ◆

When you offer a weekend package it helps to inform the customer first of the top line rate. So long as this is a reasonable rate in the first place, the relationship between the two rates will look as if you are offering a good deal.

It is vital to focus on the value of the service in relation to the rack rate, so that the temporary price promotion is seen as offering great perceived value.

There is always a debate about the wisdom of including breakfast in your room rates. Branded budget hotels do not include breakfast in their rates because they claim that customers want a choice about whether to take breakfast or not. On the other hand, Express by Holiday Inn does include it in their rate. Most small hotels and pubs with rooms seem to include it. It really depends on your market. I have found that business travellers prefer to have the choice, and if you include it in the rate you then have an argument when they don't take breakfast. Leisure travellers are most likely going to have breakfast anyway so you might as well include it.

To increase the perceived value you should only use photographic images that place you in a good position relative to your competition.

Price communication

It is helpful to appreciate that your buyer's preference can be influenced by the way that you state your prices. If you have two prices, then one is seen as being expensive and the other as cheap. Introduce a price in the middle and that is then seen as inexpensive and will attract more buyers. This is a particularly useful strategy in a wine list or on a menu. If you extend your list with some really expensive wines or dishes then you will 'drag' up the average spend, since those items near the middle are not now seen as being so expensive. You will also make fewer sales of the really low-priced items because no one likes being seen as a cheapskate!

Pricing model

It is tempting to look back to the pre-internet era as some golden age when it was easy to set your various prices for each market segment and then just take the bookings. I don't remember it quite like that. Often you would set certain rates

18 months in advance and then realise you had made an error, but there was nothing that you could do about it. At least now, with less and less paper, nothing much is fixed for very long.

Now hotel rates are a lot more transparent but I don't think we are yet at the end of the changes that will take place. Even now, we give fixed rates to companies and then are upset when they look on the internet and find lower rates being given to one-off visitors; and they have the cheek to cancel and rebook at the lower rate!

Of course fixed corporate rates still give some comfort to company financial directors and travel managers who need to know the budgeted travel costs for the coming year. The reality is that the hotel business everywhere is very seasonal, with sometimes vast fluctuations in demand patterns. Averaging out rates over 12 months for these companies will eventually become a thing of the past, and they will be treated to the same seasonal fluctuations as everyone else. That said, it is often a matter of power. If occupancies are high, the hotels make the running with rates and policies. As soon as a new hotel opens and there is too much capacity then there is the usual dogfight for occupancy.

Rate segments

Some hotels do seem to make life difficult for themselves by having literally hundreds of different rates. I understand that this sort of rate schedule, if managed effectively, can maximise each revenue opportunity as it arises. However most independent hotels need to constrain their wage bill and make everyone as multi-tasked as possible; keeping a simple tariff structure can make a contribution to this.

◆ TIP ◆

Your structure will depend to a certain extent on which markets you are trying to serve. For instance, if you think that there is potential from clients of the travel agent groups (e.g. American Express and BTI) and you want to participate in their schemes, you will need to offer a special rate. This rate will need to be at least ten per cent lower than your published rate.

Local companies often want discounts just for existing. I have never understood how ready hotels are to give away special rates to local companies without any guarantee of business. Where else can you get a discount by saying, 'I will buy more from you in the future, so can I have a discount now?' Have you considered giving them a retrospective discount at the end of the year? This way they can prove that they have more business. Sometimes a company gives you all the business they have and they are very committed to you, so why discount the price?

Another consideration is the proximity of the client's premises and the location of the competition. Evaluate carefully the likelihood of them using anywhere else. Try to avoid giving different companies rates that vary by a few pence. It makes it confusing for everyone.

A rate scheme used to look like this:

- ◆ rack rate
- ◆ consortia rates
- ◆ corporate rates
- ◆ conference rates
- ◆ group rates
- ◆ weekend rates
- ◆ special rates.

Each broad category had various subdivisions.

Much has changed in the last few years, accelerated by the transparency of the internet. It is very hard to sustain high fixed rack rates and there is much crossover between rates unless you erect the right 'hurdles' (such as full prepayment and no changes without extra cost). A scheme now might look like this:

◆ sell rate (may fluctuate daily depending upon anticipated demand);
◆ corporate rate (fixed year round rates for local businesses);
◆ group rate (varies depending upon season);
◆ weekend rate (fluctuates based upon season).

Keeping the initiative

Whatever you do, it is vital that you stay in control of your inventory and rates. Keep your pricing flexible but the closer your prices are to your customers' expectations, the less you will need to change them. You stay in charge by:

◆ Ensuring it is easy to book on-line from your website.

◆ Making sure that if you do change rates your own site always has the best deal.

◆ Maintaining your visibility via internet travel sites and hotel portals. There are plenty of good performing sites but they need constant managing and daily updating with new packages and pictures. If you aren't able to carry out this daily task, consider outsourcing the activity.

◆ Setting realistic rates in relation to your competition.

♦ Communicating well within your hotel. You definitely lose the initiative if someone puts a special rate on an internet site and forgets to tell reception about it.

Testing price points

You can do all the research possible and check the competition to destruction, but nothing will tell you your optimum room rates. The only thing you can do is test your ideas to see what nets you the most revenue. This is not so easy with rates that you have to guarantee in advance, such as corporate or group rates. For segments that you use to fill up gaps in your occupancy it is relatively easy. The internet is useful in that you can change things very quickly, so try putting together different 'packages'; say by adding dinner and entry to local attractions (although you will then have to pay commission on these extras). Use radically different room rates and see if there is any differences in take up.

Commission

Commission paid to third parties is a fact of life if you use agents to help you reach your customers. It is certainly a cost and one that should be reduced if possible. But sometimes you have to think of the alternatives, which may well be an empty bed. If you could have filled that bed at a higher net rate yourself then obviously your strategy should change. However, if you look at commission from the other end, at least you receive 90 per cent of the revenue you might well not have had in the first place and you have the opportunity to generate extra spend on drinks and dinner.

Commission payments can make a big impact on your net rates. If you use a reservation company and you get a booking through the GDS from an agent, you will be paying a reservation fee of around seven per cent, agent's commission of ten per cent plus a GDS fee, which adds up to between 20 and 30 per cent of the rate. As long as this is against a high rate then there is probably no issue. However be careful about your distribution channel when you are issuing promotional rates.

Personally I love commission payments! The higher they are the more business you have received through that source. The only difficulty is that the commission invoice can seem very large and usually arrives after the guest has left. An ideal cash flow, but maybe the commission would be more palatable if you had to pay it in advance.

Rate tactics

Request for proposal (RFPs)
Depending on how your distribution is set up, you will receive RFPs from travel agent consortia (Carlson Wagonlit, BTI, Rosenbluth, American Express, etc) and commercial organisations. If you feel that there could be business through worldwide travel agencies then you will need to submit your rates for their own-brand corporate rate programme for the following calendar year anytime from the previous June/July. You will have to pay in advance to be submitted to these agencies (anything from US$250 upwards) with no guarantee of being accepted, although these fees are refunded if you are unsuccessful.

There is really not much you can do beforehand to evaluate whether or not you will generate business through these programmes (city and airport locations do best), but it is a fair chance that you will not be accepted unless there is at least some existing traffic to the destination. Of course, once you are in the programme you can keep appropriate records.

Your rates will need to offer some level of discount (usually at least ten per cent), so be careful how this might affect the rates that you offer elsewhere.

Rate checking

One of the difficulties of maximising your revenue is understanding how the other hotels in your competitive set are behaving. Although you don't necessarily want to follow the herd, having up-to-date information will definitely help you decide on your rate strategy.

There is now technology available that will constantly monitor the web and compare various advance booking rates for hotels that you can select. Contact your reservation or representation company for details of which companies they use, or contact direct organisations such as TravelClick or RateTiger. A less costly alternative is to call up a site such as laterooms.com regularly and check what rates are being offered by your competition.

Rate parity

You will often be asked by agents and internet sites for 'rate parity'. All that they are doing is making sure that they are not undercut by other agencies that have lower rates. This is an entirely reasonable request and it makes sense to keep faith with the agencies that you are asking to distribute your rooms.

Guaranteed lowest rate

This is a completely different proposition. Some internet sites will ask you to ensure that they are offering your rooms guaranteed to be at the 'lowest rate'. This is not very helpful, since you should always be in control and make sure that your own site offers the best rates that are available. However it is not a phrase that you want to use either, since it focuses on price rather than benefits.

RevPAR

Revenue per available room (RevPAR) is a useful way of measuring your performance, particularly against your competition or industry standards. It removes the sometimes conflicting influences of occupancy and average rate and enables hotels of different sizes to be compared directly. If you are only measuring your own performance then you can just measure total revenue to see if this year was better than last. But even this can be misleading. Your revenue may have been up but maybe your occupancy was also up, with its consequent increase in costs. Maybe the extra costs are more than the increase in revenue?

To calculate revenue per available room merely take your net daily revenue and divide it by the number of rooms in your hotel. If you have already calculated the occupancy and average rate you can multiply these two together for the same outcome.

You can calculate costs (fixed and variable) on the same basis to see what the margins are. This can assist in calculating the lowest rate at which it is sensible to sell rooms to make marginal revenue.

RevPASH

If you are interested in using some yield management techniques in your restaurant you need to calculate your revenue per available seat-hour (RevPASH). This really helps you to focus on those times of the week and times of the day when revenue is weakest. To calculate this figure divide the net revenue taken in each hour by the number of seats available in the restaurant.

YIELD MANAGEMENT

Yield management is a relatively simple concept, and one that you intuitively practice anyway. What you are trying to do is maximise revenue whatever the prevailing circumstances. Where there is high demand, you try to maximise the rate from each guest. Where the demand is not so high, you try to maximise the occupancy, albeit maybe at lower rates. The idea is that you can shift the demand of those customers who are relatively price sensitive but time insensitive to off-peak times. This then clears the peak time for customers who are relatively time sensitive but price insensitive.

Rooms

To institute any strategy of maximising room yield you need information. Without it you cannot do anything. You need to be able to predict the peaks and troughs by keeping details of what happened last year, noting any planned major events in your area and by keeping an eye on developing forward reservation patterns.

A very useful measure for forward bookings is to know how many reservations you have in the books for up to, say, 90 days before arrival. This answers the question 'How are we doing?' If last year on the 30 April you had 400 leisure room nights booked for the next 90 days and this year at the same time you only have 200, then you should probably take some action!

In an ideal world you would know the specific outcomes from adjusting prices for each of your market segments (the demand elasticity). Unfortunately the hotel business is not yet that scientific and, even if it were, you can never know the reaction of your competitors; their actions usually subvert any strategy you implement. What you do know is that in the short term you cannot influence corporate or group business but that you can affect weekend and leisure guests; by how much is mostly subject to trial and error.

◆ TIP ◆

What you want to avoid is selling exactly the same facility for exactly the same price with the same conditions to different sets of customers. Everyone understands that corporate clients get a lower rate because of their buying power but two customers who are staying for the weekend having a conversation about their different prices may not be very understanding.

In the airline industry it seems more acceptable that the seat is sold at different prices, usually on the risk that you take by booking late or early. Perhaps airline seats are scarcer than hotel rooms, so customers are more forgiving? You need to try to keep stable rates at least for each day but if you cannot, then implement some restrictions.

You cannot just be arbitrary in your rate setting. Each rate needs its conditions that appeal to the segment you want. For instance you can set a Saturday rate of £125. You can also have a rate of £100 if guests stay for two nights including Saturday. What is unreasonable is to have a rate of £125 plus a rate of £100 for the same night but to try to hide the £100 rate unless the customer asks for a discount. Make logical conditions and your guests will be happy.

Although in essence yield management is a simple concept, it can become very complicated when you have a large hotel with a number of market segments and many distribution channels. There is helpful software that you can run on your property management system. But the most important factor is the human one, so never let the machine persuade you to do something that doesn't sound sensible. Intuition and gut feel are the best judges.

There are some difficulties and these need to be taken into account:

- Demand is sometimes difficult to forecast for small market segments.

- It is hard to estimate price elasticity.

- You need to keep market segments separate from each other by erecting 'hurdles'.

- Maximising capacity sometimes disguises revenue opportunities lost.

- Too many deals are difficult for staff to manage.

Restaurants

The key to maximising revenue in your restaurant is to look at maximising the revenue from the capacity. You need to look beyond measuring covers to measure revenue per available seat hour (RevPASH). The two primary variables that you have to deal with in a restaurant are customer demand and meal duration.

Controlling customer demand has its challenges. You do not know when exactly customers will arrive even if they make reservations.

 TIP

> You can request reservation guarantees by credit card and you can phone booked customers on the day to reconfirm.

If you do not take reservations, life is even more unpredictable unless you have good history and demand has remained stable. On the other hand a queue gives a steady flow at busy times.

The duration of your customers' meal is another area which is difficult to control. Some restaurants have taken to advising customers that they can have a table for, say, two hours. This seems a dreadful way to deal with an issue not always in the customers' control. It is far better to ensure that your operation functions effectively enough to allow for some control over the meal duration.

To do this you need to analyse your process all the way from arrival→greeting→seating→ordering→wine→appetizer→main course→dessert→payment→departure, standardise the procedures and evaluate all the areas where things can go wrong. To maximise your operational effectiveness you will also need to look at menu design and staff scheduling.

Differential menu pricing is difficult to implement although some restaurants do charge more at dinner than at lunch for the same item. I don't know whether customers are happy with this but the practice is not widespread, so maybe it is not that popular. The one variable that can be used effectively is time. This is why 'early bird' rates for anyone eating before 6.30pm work well. The same applies to special lunch prices.

You can do a few things to increase the yield from peak times:

◆ **Don't up-sell**: It is more important to keep to the planned meal duration and have the table reset and occupied.

◆ **No reservations**: A queue ensures better utilisation.

◆ **Narrow the menu**: Take off some lower-priced items to help average spend, and remove complicated dishes to help meal duration.

◆ **No promotions**: Not available in peak times.

◆ **Host**: Greeting and seating becomes more important.

◆ **Raise prices**: Groups might pay extra for access to a peak time.

Of course the benefits of yield management only accrue if you have the demand. But measurement of the RevPASH will give you some idea of where to apply your promotional effort.

Discounting

This is a really emotive subject. I don't really hold with the principle that what happens in the hotel industry is 'discounting' at all. To give a discount you have to have a fixed price in the first place to discount from. What we do is set prices or rates that are appropriate for each particular market segment depending on the time of the year or week. If you charge £100 for a Wednesday and £75 for a Saturday, have you discounted Saturday?

A recent study by the Cornell Center for Hospitality Research found that discounting doesn't work. What they established was that hotels that lowered their rates compared to their competition did indeed gain occupancy. What they didn't gain was higher RevPAR, so that they were actually worse off, even without taking into account the costs of running at higher occupancies.

To me this shows that you can't just take a blanket approach to prices. Each market segment has its own response to price changes. Weekend guests might respond positively to price reductions and you may well gain more in occupancy than the price reduction (this segment is reasonably price elastic). However a price reduction or discount given to government employees, for instance, is not likely to increase the volume of travel at all; revenue will then be less than before (price inelastic).

What the study also found was that holding rates when your competitors are discounting theirs might help solidify your revenues. Even raising your prices relative to your competition may lose you some occupancy but you will make up this loss by an increase in RevPAR.

To me all that this confirms is that you are on a slippery slope if you start to look at price as the main driver of business. Setting appropriate prices is vital, but this has to be based on an evaluation of your competition and your value relative to similar competitive establishments. Sometimes we can be very sensible and then along comes some very stupid competitor (often a chain property that has its price policy set at head office, usually a long way away). There is nothing that we can do about someone else's business plan. We just have to be confident in our own proposition and keep plugging away at it. Although your RevPAR is not sacrosanct, it can take years to get back to where you were if you become involved in severe discounting.

KEY POINTS

- Sometimes you have to have a strong nerve when chains make strange pricing decisions.

- The hotel business is about long-term relationships so try to avoid too much discussion about price.

- Try to keep your rate schedule as simple and realistic as possible.

- A great deal of third party internet selling is on price, mainly because there is little opportunity to establish value by differentiating on location and facilities.

- Yield management is a relatively simple concept but is always based on having useful historical information.

10

How Do You Make Systems and Data Work For You?

It is easy to drown in a sea of information, but without relevant data and systems to manage them you cannot make informed decisions. Most sales generating activities work best if they are thought through as a system.

HOW TO MEASURE CUSTOMER SATISFACTION

There are not many organisations that don't have customer satisfaction as their main priority. Even some government departments and agencies seem to be a lot more enlightened and try to focus on the 'customer'. However, without the direct stimulus of competition and a continual threat to your business it is very hard to maintain a true customer focus.

In your position you don't have any such problems. There is always someone ready and willing to take any customer of yours that is not only satisfied but also delighted. If you continually strive to 'do best what matters most', then the bottom line will be improved by your ability to charge more and your higher retention rate.

Most hotels have some sort of guest questionnaire, usually in the bedroom, with a series of tick boxes graded Excellent, Good and Poor. Unfortunately the answers you receive are virtually useless since even if the guest ticks the 'Excellent' box against 'Friendliness of reception staff' it doesn't tell you how important this is to that particular guest. If they don't care about this specific aspect then it will not have increased their commitment to your hotel. All surveys must be able to rate your performance relative to customers' priorities. (Also, the rating of 'Excellent' will depend on the customer's opinion of what is excellent, which may be different to yours.)

Why measure

Generating new customers is a difficult and expensive exercise so it is fairly obvious that we should do what we can to keep the customers that we have. There is always some natural attrition, due to a variety of factors such as moving, death, changed habits and so on, but what we don't want to do is add to this leakage by doing anything that might contribute to customers making a positive decision to try another hotel.

Customers can become dissatisfied by a number of factors which create a gap between their expectations and their experience. This gap can be created by:

◆ Promising more than you can deliver, either in a promotional offer or a sales promise.

- Procedures not being set up to meet customers' expectations.

- No full understanding of customers' needs and priorities.

- Staff not following agreed procedures at all times.

- Customer having a mistaken perception based on previous experience.

If these gaps exist it is usually not through any positive intent. No one goes out of their way to have dissatisfied customers, but it is only through measurement that it is possible to identify where your service has been below expectations.

You also need to measure customer satisfaction as a counterbalance to your own perceptions. For instance, having a full restaurant or even a full hotel does not imply that everyone is satisfied. They might be staying with you because there is no good alternative and as soon as a new hotel or restaurant opens they will all leave with a sigh of relief!

Defining customer issues

Before you can measure whether you are meeting your customers' expectations or not you have to know what is important to them. A small example: you might assume that the priorities of your weekend guests are a clean room and home-cooked food. However if you actually asked them, you might find that they rate the quality of your welcome more highly. It would therefore not be of much value if you took guests' comments on cleanliness as a measure of guest satisfaction.

First of all you need to list all the aspects of your product that add up to the customer value package. Amongst others this will include:

- bedroom accommodation
- room rates
- ease of making reservation
- check-in and out procedures
- breakfast (content and service)
- décor
- ambience
- friendliness of staff
- competence of staff
- location
- restaurant (food and service)
- cleanliness
- spa treatment availability
- entertainment

You should include things that you can control, as well as those that you can't, so that you can get a complete picture of satisfaction. Even if you can't do anything about your location at least it will be useful to know what your customers think about it.

One difficulty is that one situation does not fit all. Your different market segments will have different priorities and you need to take this into account. You should consider at least:

- corporate users
- weekend guests
- groups
- leisure users.

Finding out priorities

The difficulty for most hotels is to develop some reliable priorities for their value package at a reasonable cost. This phase is definitely an investment and you will be able to use what you find out for a few years at least. You should probably employ an outside agency to conduct some focus groups with different types of users. Focus group participants will be able to add to your initial list of items and will be encouraged by the group leader to rate all these factors with a score out of ten.

Alternatively, you can use your customers to develop the priorities for you. This will not be as helpful or as accurate since you will not find out which factors are more important than others. However you will be able to establish how important they rate certain elements of your offer. Use a semantic differential scale with seven tick boxes: 'not at all important' at one end and 'extremely important' at the other. Then list the factors that you think are priority areas for each particular segment. You could ask a few guests to help with this list, otherwise you will only be measuring what you think is important not what your guests think is important.

For instance corporate users' priorities could be:

- Bedrooms must have a large working area.
- Hotel staff must be helpful.
- Hotel staff must be friendly.
- Breakfast must be served within 30 minutes.
- Room service must be available 24 hours.
- Hotel must be flexible over early check out.

If you are interested in understanding your satisfaction rating with corporate bookers (as opposed to corporate users), then your exploratory research should probably be done by in-depth interviews with all the people that are involved in making corporate contracts. This will often not be confined to the actual booker, who may also have to consult with finance, the users, sales and marketing and purchasing. Sometimes it is a very complicated decision-making unit and you need to understand the influences of each party in the overall decision.

Once they have done this, you will have your baseline from which your customers can evaluate your actual performance.

Surveying customer satisfaction

Whenever you undertake a survey you will always be trading off the cost with the validity of the outcome. As I said earlier, questionnaires left in the rooms are almost useless, but who can afford to telephone every guest and spend half an hour on the phone? There would even be some inbuilt bias in this approach since it is unlikely that you would actually be able to speak to them all.

A compromise is actually to approach guests as they are checking out and ask them to spend a few minutes helping you before they leave. At least this way you can give the right questionnaire to the right market segment, and a personal approach will often persuade people to be helpful to you. Your questionnaire mustn't appear too daunting or else they will put it in their bag and do it later. Likely story!

Your questionnaire should use the same priority list as before only this time with a different scale of seven tick boxes.

Corporate users' priorities:

Bedroom working area is:	*too small*	☐	☐	☐	☐	☐	☐	☐	*big enough*
Hotel staff are:	*very unhelpful*	☐	☐	☐	☐	☐	☐	☐	*very helpful*
Hotel staff are:	*very unfriendly*	☐	☐	☐	☐	☐	☐	☐	*very friendly*
Breakfast service is:	*very slow*	☐	☐	☐	☐	☐	☐	☐	*very quick*
Room service availability is:	*very limited*	☐	☐	☐	☐	☐	☐	☐	*very good*
Hotel early check out is:	*very unhelpful*	☐	☐	☐	☐	☐	☐	☐	*very helpful*

This is not a perfect template for you to use but I hope you get the idea. To emphasise the point, you are trying to measure how satisfied customers are with your offer, based on *their* idea of priorities not yours.

Outcomes

The outcome of a customer satisfaction survey is to establish whether or not there are any gaps in your service. You will see the size of the gaps and the importance that customers place on them. You will be able to see what your priorities should be for making improvements. Closing small gaps in priority areas is more vital than closing large gaps in unimportant areas.

Public forums

Many internet sites now feature comments made by guests who have stayed with you. Indeed, your dissatisfied guests might post their comments on the internet rather than contact you direct. This would be an unfortunate development since these sites do not yet seem to offer hotels a 'right of reply'.

Despite safeguards, you are at the mercy of both informed and ill-informed comment, and you cannot influence the weight that potential guests give to each. There is really nothing much you can do except ensure that guests do put their positive comments on these booking sites. A questionnaire given to each guest along the lines that I have suggested here may well prompt your guests to at least highlight the 'right' areas!

USEFUL DATA TO KEEP

A database is nothing more than a collection of all the information that you keep on your customers, guests and bookers. Of course, having accumulated this data you are then under pressure to actually do something with it. So before you collect any information at all, you need to decide exactly the purpose for collecting it.

For instance you can collect a list of all your past guests but if you don't then send them details of your special promotions then all you have done is waste paper or space on your hard drive. Conversely, if you decide that you want to promote your hotel to the local business community, before you can start you will need to make a list of the most useful bookers.

I suggest that you need to collect data on the following:

◆ guests;
◆ restaurant customers;
◆ corporate bookers and meeting planners;
◆ travel and other agents;
◆ referral and joint venture partners.

Guests

If you have a computerised Property Management System (PMS) or even a web-based system which avoids the need for you to buy expensive hardware, then it will automatically accumulate information on all your past guests. If you put the system in new then you will be asked by the supplier to specify what type of information you want to keep and what segmentation to use. If you still use paper and an eraser for your room management (and there is nothing wrong with that) then you can use your registration forms to collect the information and put the details into a binder or use a programme like MS Access. I would recommend that the registration form contains the following information for each guest:

- arrival date;
- departure date;
- name and address including postcode;
- telephone;
- e-mail (plus confirmation that you have permission to use it);
- rate paid;
- room number;
- date reservation made;
- a code for guest's reason for stay: either business (split between individual/corporate contract/meeting) or leisure (split between individual/group or tour/special promotion/wedding);
- a code for the source of the reservation (direct from guest/agent plus name/company plus name/own site/third party site and name).

Your guest registration form now has all the information you need to help you get back in touch with the guests, but also accumulate some statistics about where your reservations originate and which companies or agents give you significant business. With this detail you can decide to carry out some extra promotion based on firm knowledge about which sources are working and which aren't.

What the registration form will not do is help you find out if there is more business from any particular guest source. For each guest you need an answer to the questions, 'What is the reason you are staying here?' and, 'Are there more potential guests where you came from?' These questions are two of the most powerful tools at your disposal. With the answers you have a constant supply of follow-up actions.

Your split between leisure and business will enable you to carry out different promotions. Leisure guests who are happy with their stay may well come back again in a low season period if you give them a big enough incentive. The only issue is keeping your list 'clean': you can obtain some software that deletes people who have moved and/or died but it may be less costly and just as effective to only mail those guest who have stayed during the previous two years.

Your business guests may not be that useful a list. These guests may well be staying with you because they were put there by their company so they have no discretion. However you may have a lot of individual business guest, who make their own decisions, and you will definitely want to keep communicating with them. The information you collected on the registration form or through your PMS will give you the necessary information to isolate the different types of guests. You may be competing with chain or franchise hotels that operate what they call loyalty schemes – have you thought about such a scheme for your hotel?

Is there a place for loyalty schemes?

What exactly is a loyalty scheme? I think that this whole concept has become a bit distorted and lost its way. It is manifest in the myriad number of 'loyalty' programmes operated by car hire firms, chain hotels and airlines. Frequent users are rewarded by points based on their spend, on the assumption that the most frequent users are the most loyal. This is not necessarily the case.

There are two major problems with these loyalty schemes. Firstly, customers should be loyal to a hotel not to a 'scheme'. Why would you want to insert something between you and your customer? Secondly, by giving away tokens you are effectively buying something that should be given for nothing. And if you are buying it, it is not loyalty (loyalty is defined as 'unconditional and unwavering allegiance …').

From what I hear, some of the companies that operate these schemes regret getting into them in the first place, but cannot now stop. Because customers stay for rewards, they also leave for rewards and the points allocated then become a cost to the business, with no identifiable change in behaviour.

◆ **TIP** ◆

Look in your own wallet and see how many so-called loyalty cards you have, probably at least two from competing supermarkets where you take the rewards because they are offered. Do you really change your behaviour because of the rewards?

A lot of organisations put a great deal of effort into their schemes. In my opinion this is looking in completely the wrong direction. What they should surely be doing is providing the sort of value and benefits (customer satisfaction) that ensure that customers keep coming back because of your hospitality, not your 'bribe'.

Guests are loyal (don't switch) for a number of reasons, both to do with your hotel and their own needs for belonging. They keep coming back because they make some internal evaluation of what they would lose if they switched to another hotel. So if you keep doing what you do, the loyal customer will keep coming back because you meet his or her needs. Therefore in some respects you need to do less, not more, for your loyal customers!

This is not to say that you shouldn't reward loyal customers. But before you do, you need to find out what it is that made them committed to your hotel in the first place, and reinforce that aspect. Also consider how you can reinforce your own loyalty to these committed customers who are the foundation of a secure business.

Restaurant customers

If you have an EPOS system in your restaurant that is linked to your PMS then you will have the facility to accumulate information on your restaurant customers. You will have their times and dates of visit and how much they spend. What you will not have is their name, address and e-mail. Again there is no point in collecting this information unless it is part of a communication strategy that you have developed to generate more frequent visits.

To encourage restaurant customers to want to develop a relationship with you and give you permission to e-mail them (by far the lowest cost solution), you need to offer them something in return. Membership schemes of one sort or another can work well, even if it is a lunch club, a literary circle or just a pudding club.

Membership schemes

A membership scheme is not the same as a loyalty scheme. With membership you are tapping into people's desire to belong to something. Look in your wallet and you will find any number of cards that try to tap into this natural feeling.

For an independent hotel there is less benefit for bedroom sales since leisure guests are likely to be infrequent and corporate guests use you for practical reasons. The main use is likely to be to help generate extra business for your restaurant.

Benefits

♦ Group best users together: you can target your efforts to where the benefit is. You can also segment the list and isolate special groups (e.g. retired people).

♦ Promote less popular times: you can give special incentives for lunch times or early week evenings.

♦ Sell special events: this helps generate extra revenue for special events such as wine tasting, gourmet evenings or food promotions.

♦ Improve referrals: people like to tell other people about 'clubs' they are part of.

- Opportunity for communication: helps you set up two-way dialogue with your members, which is great for both positive and negative feedback.

What to include

Your scheme should be designed around what you are trying to achieve. Keep you objectives firmly in mind. Remember that you are trying to achieve two things together:

- Making people feel good about being part of your 'club'.
- Generating more revenue than you would have done without the 'club'.

So you will be arranging some activities that are merely rewards (coach trip to the races with you) and some that will drive revenue (early evening dining discount). Some more examples are:

- Invitations to special member only events – wine tasting, pig roasts, lunch lectures etc.

- Special promotions – free wine with two meals Monday to Thursday, special lunch menu etc.

- Offers from third parties – special offer at local spa, flower shop etc.

- Outings for members only – local gardens, sporting events etc.

Fees

It is probably optimistic to expect people to pay a fee to join your club. And would you want the membership to be circumscribed by the payment of a fee? You really want as many likely prospects as possible in your scheme, so the more the better. However, if you develop a really good scheme then you could segment into a free (silver?) section and a (gold?) section with additional benefits for the payment of a small annual fee. Keep in mind the costs and software associated with running a membership scheme that is set up to collect fees.

How to develop

You can generate members for your scheme in two ways. The first is your internet site, where you can put an application form on your restaurant page. Keep it as simple as possible and maybe just collect full name, postcode and e-mail address. Lay out the benefits of the club clearly and possibly offer a special offer as a first stage reward for joining and giving you their e-mail address.

Secondly, put together a simple leaflet and distribute around the hotel and restaurant. Give a leaflet with all bills. Mail to your current list and consider door-to-door distribution in your catchment area.

Corporate bookers and meeting planners

If you are in a business-related area, corporate bookers and meeting planners are likely to be the two most valuable groups of bookers (some contacts will of course book both rooms and meeting facilities) that you deal with on a day-to-day basis and with whom you can establish a personal relationship. To keep this data you will need a separate file to the one that you use for guests and customers. This information can only come from your own input and will not be generated automatically by any in-house system.

If you have a large number of these contacts that you are working on, you can use a proprietary software system such as ACT! or Goldmine. Alternatively, some PMS systems have a contact management option. You can also use MS Access, although this does not have the features of a specially developed program. As I said before, even if you use an A4 folder with a page for each contact, just having the information will be a great bonus and will put you ahead of some of your competitors.

If you are trying to develop business from the local area for the first time then you will really have to start at the beginning by driving around and making a note of organisations that look as if they might have potential. You can then phone up the company and ask to speak to the person who books local accommodation or meetings. From this conversation you should be able to work out whether there is potential for your hotel or not. (Details of the sales process are in Chapter 4.)

This is the minimum information that you need to accumulate for each organisation:

- organisation name
- address
- telephone
- website
- company activity
- number of employees
- contact person/s
- e-mail
- how decisions are made (who is involved?)
- how bookings are made (direct/GDS/booker etc)
- hotels used in area
- total room nights p.a. booked by company
- your potential share of total
- other potential business (meetings/lunch/Christmas etc)
- follow-up needed/agreed
- room rate proposed/agreed
- history (including actual usage)

Of course this is not a one-off exercise. You will need to keep your eyes open constantly for organisations moving into the area. As well as driving around there is a lot of information available from local newspapers (editorial and recruitment sections), commercial transfer agents and Business Link.

Travel and other agents

Before you start to generate huge files on travel intermediaries you need to decide what you are going to do with the information. You may find that you receive a number of reservations from a travel agent in San Francisco. What are you going to do, now that you have the details? If your hotel is bookable through GDS then it would seem sensible to accumulate details of the source of your overseas reservations to see if your investment has been worthwhile. If this is as far as you want to go then you can just collect basic details and rely on the commission claims sent by your reservation partner.

If, however, you want to find out from the agent why they are using your hotel and whether or not there is more business available, you will need their telephone and e-mail for follow up. You can use your system to record names, addresses, contact numbers and recommended follow up by yourself.

Although there are hundreds of specialist agencies such as venue finding and hotel booking agencies, it is likely that you will find yourself having a positive relationship with no more than a handful. Even if you started off being very active, telephoning them all and doing the correct follow up, each has their own specialism, which will rule you out for one reason or another.

◆ TIP ◆

These agencies can be a good source of business, and you should try to develop a good relationship with the individual bookers. Make sure that you keep details of exactly what business they are likely to use your hotel for.

Referral and joint venture partners

These two groups can produce a lot of business for you if you are active with them. However it is sometimes very difficult to measure when a relationship has worked. By referral contacts I mean those complementary organisations in your area that are likely to be asked about local accommodation. These can be other suppliers of accommodation who perhaps are small and get booked up quickly, or local attractions that generate a large number of visitors, some of who may need accommodation.

A joint venture partner would be other businesses that supply products or services that are complementary to your hotel. These could be local florists, day spas, cycle rental or even restaurants if you only supply breakfast.

All the principals in these organisations need to be kept on your database, so that you can write down exactly what your relationship is with them and what follow up is needed. To decide what to write down, assume that you are handing the project over to someone else and they have no clue what you are talking about. It is vital to measure the outcome from any promotion that you carry out. If you are distributing your hotel leaflets to your colleagues in local bed and breakfasts (for overflow and dinner business), make sure that you put a special code on the leaflets so that you can thank them for the business.

Update your database with the numbers of referrals made so that you can make a good plan for the following year.

IMPLEMENT SYSTEMS FOR AN EASIER LIFE

Within your hotel you already have plenty of systems. I would guess that most of them are associated with housekeeping, the restaurant and the kitchen. Some of them will have developed as a result of custom and practice, and some you will have set down in writing after consulting your team.

However, you probably have few written systems that govern your sales and marketing activity. This is a shame since there is so much money to be made by implementing systems that can take care of business development even when you are not there. For example, how often do you worry that the person answering the phone will not be as thorough as you are in chasing the sale? You need to think of the absence of a system as a potential 'leak'. If it was the roof you would put in a monitoring system to make sure that it didn't leak, and if it did you would make every effort to repair it as soon as you spotted it.

◆ TIP ◆

Sales opportunities leak just like roofs. It is amazing how much of this business potential is not capitalised upon. Of course, if you have a really committed and motivated team you are half way to ensuring that opportunities are not lost. It should be in everyone's interest to make sure that revenue is maximised.

Everything you do is a system. A system is made up of a series of steps, in a specific order, and with a designated outcome. Tying your shoelaces is a system and so is driving a car. The steps have to be learnt at some stage; we learnt them because we wanted to achieve the designated outcome. To take the driving analogy a bit further, some of us pick up some bad habits and we really should go back to school and take an advanced course.

The same applies to our sales systems. From time to time we should analyse them and change the steps so that they deliver the results we want. For example, I was working with a client who had a system for promoting Christmas parties – he put some very poor quality leaflets in a rack in the reception area and wondered why his advanced sales were not very impressive!

He managed to improve sales fourfold just by changing the system – a better quality leaflet was put in all outbound mailed confirmations and the party special was mentioned over the phone to all inbound callers. I know this is not a very impressive marketing campaign but it does show that by making small changes to a system that is not delivering you can experience improved results.

Every marketing system can be improved to generate better results. Take a look at these 'systems':

- sales development
- inbound calls for rooms
- inbound calls for functions
- restaurant menus
- brochure and tariff enquiries
- referrals
- testimonials
- promoting special events
- up-selling in the restaurant.

Sales development

This is definitely an area where you cannot afford to be haphazard. Whenever you carry out any sales development activity these steps all have to be carried out so that you achieve your objective. It should work like this.

♦ **Target:** Establish where you are likely to find groups of prospects that are in the market for your service.

♦ **Reach:** Make contact with these prospects using any of the channels highlighted in Part 2 (direct, contact, direct mail, advertising etc).

♦ **Record:** Put into a database all those prospects that respond to your offer, provide their contacts details and are in a position to decide to buy your service.

♦ **Follow up:** Proactive follow up (with special offers and guarantees if necessary) is the key to success and may have to be done a minimum of five times. Be persistent but also know when to call it a day.

♦ **Track:** Keep records of what works so that you can change tack or keep doing more of the same.

Inbound calls for rooms

Hopefully, as a result of all the actions that you have taken, your phone will ring. This has so far cost you a lot of money but if business is booked then it will all have been worthwhile. But, as I mentioned before, it is possible for these opportunities to leak from the business. If you take the call personally then you won't put the phone down until you have secured the business at the most advantageous rate for the day, even if it means a discount off your normal rates. Are you convinced that the rest of the team will do as well?

The only way to guarantee that these incoming calls are handled efficiently and effectively is to institute a system. This system is based on having a logical script in place that everyone follows, irrespective of who they are (see Chapter 4, page 122). Having a script does not mean that you want everyone to read from it but you do want them to follow it. So long as anyone who answers the phone is trained and has practised then it won't sound like a script. It doesn't seem as though George Clooney has a script, but he most certainly does!

Inbound calls for functions

I remember one hotel I worked with couldn't understand why their wedding business was down by 50 per cent. It was a while before the manager realised that the duty manager who took most of the calls didn't like working on Saturdays! Obviously there was no system for evaluating the number of incoming enquiries, recording the correct details on a profile, following up appropriately and measuring the outcomes, both positive and negative. Again there is a need for a script, not least so that all the right information is recorded for subsequent follow up.

How many times have you been handed a message on a scrap of paper without the caller's name or with an incomplete telephone number? You should also not be embarrassed about sitting in on some of the calls so that you can see for yourself how it is working. Also set up formal meetings with all those responsible for handling the calls to evaluate how the process is working. Maybe even call some prospects yourself to check on how their call was handled by your team. Whatever system you devise, it is vital that it is written down and followed. Buy-in from the team can be improved if they devise the system themselves.

Restaurant menus

It may seem a bit exaggerated to call a menu a 'system', but when you think about it, it is a series of steps in a specific order with a designated outcome. I have seen some very complicated menu systems with, for instance, a potential diner being offered an à la carte menu, a special fixed price option and a special 'menu gourmand' all at the same time. This has obviously not been thought through from the customer's point of view nor analysed to maximise revenue from a yield aspect. Your menus need to be designed to deliver your desired outcome.

◆ TIP ◆

You need to consider the demand and the target markets in each of the 14 dining periods during the week. The potential business on Monday lunchtime is likely to be different from that on Saturday evening and the menu offered should reflect this.

Consider both the items offered and the prices, and take into account the costs of producing the food for a limited number of early week customers. Friday and Saturday are usually high demand periods, so there is no need to keep on the menu some of the cheaper items that will have worked well at Tuesday lunch.

You also need to look at the layout of the menu itself, how the descriptions sound, how much jargon is used and whether you have used some French words (e.g. *jus, lardon* etc) in an English menu. The way that the menu is printed and presented will also have an impact on the sales. Do you have a separate dessert, coffee and liqueur menu and is the wine selection included with the menu? All these decisions need to be made in association with the staff who are going to implement the system, so that they are part of the process that achieves the designated outcome.

Brochure and tariff enquiries

We covered incoming calls in Chapter 4, but the follow up of these relatively vague enquiries is often very poor. Mostly this is because those people making the enquiries often work full-time and you can only reach them in the evening. So the follow-up task has to be allocated to someone who works during this period. On the other hand many of these enquiries now come by e-mail, which does make the follow up easier.

Most of these enquirers generally have enough information available to them through your internet site, so any telephone enquiry should be taken as an invitation to enter into some sort of dialogue with them. Your system for dealing with these enquiries should include an evaluation of the rate that you are going to offer, of course based on your yield management strategy.

Sometimes though, and particularly for a weekend reservation, it is just a matter of a responsible person phoning back and offering some additional incentive, such as champagne or breakfast. Even though there is a general decline in these sorts of research enquiries due to the amount of information available on the internet, it is important to have a watertight system for converting the enquiries that you do receive.

Referrals

A referral is not the same as word-of-mouth advertising, which happens when one of your customers mentions your hotel or restaurant in a casual conversation. A referral system is part of a process that you put in place to generate recommendations. Referrals are powerful because they come from someone who has experienced your hotel and is impressed enough to want others to experience it also. The other benefit of referrals is that the person giving a referral becomes much more loyal to you.

Excellent customer service is of course the foundation of a steady source of referrals. Without it no one will recommend you, but even with it you will not generate referrals without making a system. There are three main groups from which you can generate referrals.

Customers

Referrals from your customers are powerful because they are putting their reputation on the line by recommending you to their friends and contacts. So in a sense they have just as much to lose as you.

◆ TIP ◆

Your customers are actually very keen to give referrals because it makes them feel good. They are seen to be divulging a secret that only they know. So long as you look after the new customer everyone is a winner.

You need to prompt your customers into giving referrals, both by asking for them and by being known to look after anyone who is referred. But you can't just ask for a referral without putting the request into context. For instance, if Dave is a good corporate booker and he is on the committee of the Chamber of Commerce then you might say to him, 'Dave, I understand that you are on the committee of the Chamber.' When he confirms it you could then say, 'Is there anyone on the committee who might also need local accommodation?' He might then think of one or two of his colleagues who he could approach. It may not be many but at least he is likely to do it, since you have given him a frame of reference.

There are a few opportunities that arise when you can ask if the customer knows any of their contacts that could benefit from your service. For instance, when a customer needs a favour, when they have made a mistake and you have helped them out, or when they have taken the trouble to thank you for what you have done for them.

Complementary suppliers

Depending upon your local circumstances and location you will have a number of local suppliers that you work with on a day-to-day basis. These could be tourist attractions, restaurants, other hotels, bed and breakfasts, shops, hairdressers or cycle rental. This can be made into an informal network, with you as the focus.

If you are a wedding venue then you have a ready-made group that includes limousine companies, florists, photographers, marquee suppliers, dress hire, entertainment agencies and wedding planners. Even if you don't have a wedding fayre you can arrange a networking or social event and make sure that the principals from these companies are on the distribution list for your newsletter or are members of your dining club.

If you recognise a referral from any of your associates then make sure that you send them a thank you note. If you receive a lot from a particular supplier then send them an appropriate gift. What you shouldn't do is make a formal payment system for a referral, since this is contrary to the principles of loyalty. To make a start you should make sure that you make some referrals since generally you have to give to get.

Local contacts

There is another group of local 'movers and shakers' who, while they may not use your hotel very much, can be very influential. If they are convinced that you have a good reputation and they know a little about you, they may be convinced to give a referral. This group can include your neighbours, the mayor, small business owners, lawyers, architects, accountants and politicians. It is a relatively disparate group but they could be interested in a sporting or a literary lunch in your hotel. You could also put them on your distribution list for special events and send them details of your dining club. If you get to know them you may be able to send them referrals, which may encourage them to do the same for you.

Testimonials

It is very rewarding to receive letters or e-mails from your happy customers, but how many have you actually got in proportion to your total number of customers, and how useful are the ones you have? 'Thank you for a very pleasant stay,' is a testimonial that just won't cut it with the average sceptical media-savvy consumer.

Unfortunately, your prospects expect you to wax lyrical about your product and although they might believe you there is so much hype around that you need to do something to overcome their natural scepticism.

◆ TIP ◆

Testimonials from satisfied customers are one of the most powerful tools that you can use in your promotional strategy. They operate just like PR; a testimonial is not *you* saying that you are wonderful, but a third party endorsing the quality of your service and the value of the experience.

If you don't want to sit and wait for the odd letter to arrive, you have to set up a system to generate testimonials. Whatever you do, don't confuse customer service research with soliciting testimonials. In the former you are looking for anonymous analysis, whereas in the latter you want to know exactly who is prepared to put their reputation behind your product. Here are some ideas for your testimonial system:

- **Don't delay**: Don't leave it too long to ask for a testimonial. For weekend guests, talk to them around the time that they are checking out on Sunday morning. For meeting planners, catch them just as they are appreciating the euphoria of a hassle-free meeting and the congratulations of the managing director.

- **Make it specific**: Ensure that the testimonial is specific, particularly with reference to your positioning. If your main pitch for weekends is your quiet location, then make sure that comments on the lack of noise are included. You can do this by asking questions such as, 'How far do you think we go in living up to our claim to offer a quiet location for a relaxing weekend?'

- **Get personal**: If possible, take a picture of your satisfied customers. Also make sure that they give their personal details and most importantly their permission for you to use what they say. Most people are flattered, but you still need to ask.

Testimonials can be used in variety of places, particularly on your website. Don't put them all together on one page but intersperse them appropriately in the text on the different product pages. Testimonials are also very powerful when included in your brochures and in any direct mail letter.

Promoting special events

Whenever you are promoting special events you need to follow the system outlined on page 270. However this is a general outline, and it could be useful to set down some specific actions that you can take.

Here is an example of a system that you could develop for promoting Christmas parties:

◆ **February**: Whole team, including chef, to evaluate last year's event and agree changes for next time. Include evaluation of pricing and the competition's offering so that you can come up with a distinctive and exciting offer.

◆ **June**: Decide what the target markets are, how they are going to be reached, what booking incentives to offer and what type and quantity of leaflets and posters are needed. Draft menu and prices and print on A4, or e-mail to early enquiries.

◆ **July**: Agree final pricing and menu content. Arrange printing based on what you have planned to do with leaflets. Put details plus booking form on website. Arrange listing with party promoters.

- **August:** Send out leaflets to enquiries already received. Offer incentive for bookings received before end of October.

- **September:** Send out press release to local media contacts. Send out letter and leaflets to last year's customers and prospect list offering early booking incentive. Carry out door-to-door distribution to shops in local high street, professional services firms and clubs and associations. Organise direct mailing to wider list from Chamber of Commerce. Put details on A-board at the hotel. Take leaflets to local networking events.

- **October:** Follow up all potential contacts who have registered an interest and not made a booking. Invite group from local paper, maybe free of charge if in early December (can be good for relationship in rest of year?).

- **November:** Final follow up with contacts that haven't committed. Try and find out why alternative venues have been booked so that you can include in post-event evaluation.

- **December:** At the functions get the DJ or the MC to go round and collect every participant's business card for a prize draw.

- **January:** Mail every participant with an offer to come back in January and February for a really low-cost buffet and disco as a thank you.

Other events have similar characteristics, particularly with regard to planning. A murder mystery weekend, for instance, will need just as much or maybe more planning. Your goal of a successful and profitable event will be reached by dividing the whole process into a number of easily manageable steps and allocating responsibility to appropriate members of your team.

If you put all your events for the year onto a list you will have made another system!

Up-selling in the restaurant

There is so much money to be made from creative up-selling in the restaurant that you will surely want to implement a system if you don't have one already. Part of the system is a good incentive scheme based on the Key Performance Indicators (see page 115) of the waiting staff. Beyond this you will want to ensure that the service system and the menu construction gives appropriate opportunities to generate extra revenue.

The wine list needs to have a good range of wines, including if appropriate, some more expensive ones. If it is suitable to your restaurant the dessert menu must include a full range of coffees, liqueur coffees and dessert wines so that the staff have something to sell. The menu also needs some special dishes, particularly on Friday and Saturday when customers may be open to an enhanced experience.

KEY POINTS

♦ All your future actions will be determined by the information you collect on your past successes.

♦ Collecting customers' opinions is only useful if you have a reference point for their evaluation.

♦ Don't collect data unless you are going to do something with it. It will soon pass its sell by date.

♦ Generating extra revenue is too important to be left to chance. Systems ensure that everyone follows the same path, even when you are not present.

11

What Tactics Can You Use To Develop Revenue?

It is vital to focus on a few very clear objectives. You can't do everything at once. As you chase new prospects it is easy to forget the amount of money to be made from your current customers.

CUSTOMER EVALUATION

Often you will be exhorted to spend time on the top 20 per cent of customers who will probably generate 80 per cent of your revenue. This is a very simplistic approach, which needs further exploration. In fact, if this were the case in your hotel I would quietly panic! Customers are fickle and you never know when they will decide that your hotel does not meet their needs.

If you find that you have a number of very large suppliers, you need to put a lot of effort into developing other clients to redress the balance. You need to look at the vast majority of your customers and divide them into those that can be developed and those that are unlikely to grow.

Customer share

We all know that it is less costly to sell to existing customers than to new customers. You need to make sure that you have initiatives in place that will capture a greater share of business from customers that you already have:

◆ Find out how much they spend on accommodation so that you can work out your share of their expenditure. How can you persuade them to use you more?

◆ Find out who else they buy from and ascertain exactly why they use somewhere else. Can you provide any service or amenity that would satisfy more of their needs?

◆ Find out what else they need apart from rooms. Do they need meeting space, or do they entertain customers for lunch, or maybe they have an annual corporate event or a Christmas party?

◆ Persuade them to upgrade to better rooms or take more expensive menus for their functions.

◆ Don't spend too much time on a customer when you have established that you get most of the available business from that customer; but don't ignore them either!

Lifetime value

Assessing the lifetime value of your clients is key to ensuring that you don't think short-term when you consider business development. To develop your marketing budget properly you need to know:

♦ the lifetime revenue from each new customer;
♦ how much it costs to acquire a new customer.

Of course you need to be selective and consider first your most valuable customers. This may well be regular restaurant guests and corporate clients booking rooms and/or meeting rooms. However it might still be a valuable exercise if you have a high repeat ratio for your weekend guests.

How to calculate lifetime revenue

As an example, let's look at a corporate booker using your hotel regularly for weekday accommodation and meetings. Assume that they use five rooms per week at £60 (net), then the annual revenue is £15,600. Add to this revenue, say, two meetings a year and various lunches and dinners and the total revenue may be £19,000. Assume that each company stays for around five years at this level then we are looking at £95,000.

You can try the same exercise for each customer and each restaurant guest, making sure that you take into account the natural attrition rate.

How to calculate customer acquisition costs

This is not a particularly scientific exercise but will give you a good place to start. Firstly, look at last year's total marketing costs and divide them by the number of new customers you did business with. You will need to separate these marketing costs between restaurant, weekend guests and corporate clients, so that the sums are as accurate as possible. If you spent £50,000 on brochures, sales staff salaries, expenses and entertaining and generated ten new corporate customers, then the costs of acquiring each new customer would be £5,000.

What does all this mean?

Do you think it is expensive if each new corporate client costs you £5,000 to acquire? Maybe it is if you only look at the annual revenue of £19,000. But remember that you don't have to spend this money again on this client. If you do everything right and service the client booker as they wish, then the overall cost is only £5,000 compared to the £95,000 they will spend over the projected four years. And 5.3 per cent is probably not an unreasonable marketing cost.

INCREASING REVENUE

As I said earlier, it is less expensive to generate extra revenue from your current customers than spend time, effort and money on finding new customers. But you still need to find new customers, if only to replace the 20–30 per cent that leave you for no particular reason that you can do much about. But do not forget the customers who have stopped using you because you have neglected them.

The interesting aspect of these tactics is the impact that improvements in all areas can have on your top line revenue. If you have ten per cent more customers, a ten per cent better average rate, and customers spending money with you ten per cent more often, then due to the compounding of the increases, your revenue will increase by over 30 per cent.

There are five major strategies that you can use to develop additional revenue for your hotel, and below we explore some tactics for each:

◆ Increase the number of leads.
◆ Convert leads to customers.
◆ Increase the number of transactions.
◆ Increase the average rate/spend.
◆ Improve customer retention.

Increase the number of leads

It is your marketing activity that generates interest in your hotel, and you have to find a range of activities that work for you. New leads are the lifeblood of any commercial organisation and without them your business will naturally deteriorate. The many possibilities for generating sales leads are expanded upon in detail in Part 2 but they are listed here as a reminder:

◆ telephone sales
◆ direct sales
◆ networking
◆ direct mail
◆ e-mail
◆ newsletters
◆ advertising
◆ media relations
◆ internet site.

Convert leads to customers

Once you have a steady stream of leads, you need to convert these into customers. As soon as you have managed to do this, you have the opportunity to impress them enough for them to become advocates and ambassadors for your hotel. Here are a few tactics:

- **Ask for the sale**: Sometimes we forget that this is all it takes.

- **Be persistent**: It often takes more than one encounter with a prospect to convert them to a customer. Don't give up until you have made at least five contacts (phone/e-mail/letter etc).

- **Have good systems**: These are expanded in Chapter 10 under 'Implement systems for an easier life' (pages 268–280).

- **Sales training**: Train all your team to pick up on all the leads that come in, whether these are by phone, personal visits or mail.

- **Give guarantee**: Sometimes people are reluctant to take that first step. Make it so that they have nothing to lose.

- **Pre-qualify**: Make sure that all the leads you generate are from prospects that have the willingness and the means to spend money with you.

- **Make first sale easy**: Think of the lifetime value of each prospect, and then do something to make it easy for them to make the first purchase. Make a special offer for one room for a potential corporate client as a trial. If they like it they will make another booking, and then you may get the contract.

Increase the number of transactions

Your current customers are your biggest asset and they represent the most cost-effective opportunity to generate extra revenue, whether it is for your hotel rooms, your restaurant or your leisure centre. There are probably hundreds of things you can do but here are a few to get you thinking.

- **Promotions**: Current guests are always receptive to special promotions, whether for rooms or food. Think of special menus or prices particularly for the early week lull.

- **Bounce-backs**: As guests leave your hotel or restaurant, give them a voucher entitling them to a special offer as a 'valued guest'.

- **Newsletters**: Develop an interesting newsletter and a good database and you will have the ultimate tool for reaching your customers.

- **Timed coupons**: Whenever you make an offer or special promotion always put a time limit on it. Action is what you want to stimulate.

- **Membership scheme**: Your really committed customers will be in your scheme and will be very receptive to inducements to stay more often or use your restaurant more frequently.

- **Dates/occasions**: Collect data on your customers' anniversaries and send them a special offer a few weeks beforehand.

- **Cross selling**: Receptionists have a unique opportunity to promote dinner on check-in, or to give out drinks vouchers for the bar.

Increase the average rate/spend

This is a very powerful lever to generate extra revenue. Whatever the size of your operation there is always some opportunity to persuade your customers to spend more. They will not do it unless they want to, and will probably be grateful that you gave them the chance. How many times have you wanted to be persuaded to have that chocolate dessert, only to have the server say, 'Would you like the bill now?' Coming up with ideas is a great opportunity for a team exercise.

- **Package products together**: Put together an in-room movie plus ice cream offer. Offer dinner, bed and breakfast (DBB) rates at weekends.

- **'Bump up' the order**: Imagine if half your bar customers purchased a bowl of nuts or crisps.

- **Reduce low-priced products**: On busy nights in a restaurant take off the low-priced items that work at lunchtime.

- **Up-sell**: Incentivise receptionists to up-sell to an executive room.

- **Tailor the product**: Fill the mini-bar with items based on previous purchase history.

Improve customer retention

It doesn't really need to be said, but you just cannot afford to lose customers once you have them. Often they leave you through neglect rather than any negative customer experience, but there are a great number of actions that you can take to keep them committed to you.

- **Customer service**: They won't stay at all without great customer service, but constant attention to detail will keep them coming back.

- **Under promise and over deliver**: Always a great philosophy. Give something unexpected such as a bottle of wine in the room for your weekend guests.

- **Referrals**: Customers who give referrals are more committed to you now that they are your advocates.

- **Communicate regularly**: Keep in touch with e-mails, news-letters and maybe a hand-written thank you card.

- **Ask them for regular feedback**: People love it when you ask them for help.

- **Tell them about new products**: Ask your regular guests for help in defining new elements of your product.

- **Follow up and follow up again**: Make a plan to contact all your regular bookers and guests.

- **Speed stuns**: Set some tough standards for your reply to enquiries and your response to orders.

KEY POINTS

- Knowing the proportion of a client's spend that you get now is a powerful tool for planning future sales activity.

- Establishing the likely lifetime value of all your clients will help you decide how much money and effort to put into relationship building.

- Small improvements in average spend, combined with custo-mers spending more often will have a tremendous impact on the bottom line.

- Making sure that you keep your current customers should be your most important goal.

12

Planning Your Marketing Activity

Although the marketing action plan is the most important document in the hotel, there is no point in measuring its usefulness by weight. A one-page document might be more insightful than one that contributes to the destruction of the rain forest! Whatever you plan, make it workable and realistic.

WHAT IS LEFT TO DO?

You will not be surprised to learn, if you have read the rest of this book, there is very little left for you to do to prepare your marketing plan. This whole book is, in essence, the preparation for a marketing plan, and you have actually now done most of what is needed.

It is now a case of putting all the information into order, making some decisions based on your competitive analysis, and deciding on some priority action areas. Unfortunately I can't help since you are the one that knows and understands your situation. If I made any prescription I could be accused of malpractice for making a diagnosis before evaluating the symptoms!

Why is it that very few individual hotels actually produce a marketing plan? It is common practice in chain properties and they find them tremendously beneficial, so why is the practice not followed generally? This does not only apply to hotels; very few small to medium businesses take time to think about where they are and where they want to be.

> Research shows that companies that have written goals are much more successful than those that don't.

Later on I will include a list of those items that you can include in your plan, but whatever you do, keep it simple and short.

How to do it

One of the hardest tasks to accomplish is to turn your goals into reality. This is particularly difficult if these goals stay in your head and do not become part of the business process. The idea of a marketing plan is to commit these goals to paper and put some figures behind them so that everyone in your team can share in evaluating whether or not these goals are being reached. Sales activity plans and financial budgets need regular attention, so that you can make modifications based on changes to the market or fluctuations in your performance.

To make sales and marketing plans of any sort work you need to ensure that:

- You set aside uninterrupted time with your team to develop your plan.

- Someone with fresh eyes takes a look at your business. Maybe you can hire a consultant for half a day, or ask a good client to sit with you while you hammer out the strategy. New ideas and directions are what you need.

- Those responsible for achieving the goals must be involved in making the plans. Involve reception and food service staff as well as the kitchen and housekeeping.

- All goals must be assessed to see if they are SMART:
  Specific – exactly what needs to be achieved in figures and what channels to be used
  Measurable – will you be able to assess whether or not the goal was achieved?
  Achievable – unrealistic goals usually defeat their purpose
  Relevant – is the goal relevant to your product and the target market?
  Time bound – all goals need to have a time set by which they have to be achieved

- If the goals you agree need skills that are not yet well developed in your hotel, then plan and budget the relevant training.

- Regular monthly meetings are scheduled with everyone involved in implementing the plan to review it and check that all the actions have been carried out. Update the plan with anything that you have learned, and carry this forward so that you always have a 12-month rolling plan. This prevents the annual pain!

- Keep checking the competition at regular intervals.

MARKETING PLAN FORMAT

As I said earlier, if you have read through the whole book so far you will already have considered most issues that are raised in any marketing plan. Your action plan is about how to turn your revenue goals into reality. It will include separate consideration of your:

◆ rooms
◆ meeting space
◆ bars
◆ restaurants
◆ leisure facilities.

It is vital to come up with new ideas, even if what you did last year worked. It is your responsibility to come up with innovative ideas, both for your services and for your marketing activities. If anything didn't work, then change it. In essence, developing a marketing plan is a five-stage process that answers these questions:

◆ Where are we now?
◆ Where do we want to be?
◆ What do we want to change?
◆ How are we going to get there?
◆ What are the local opportunities?

You can make the development of a marketing plan as detailed as you wish. What I have outlined here is a relatively straightforward format that will put you far ahead of your competition and provide the platform for team consensus.

Where are we now?

This section is designed to accumulate all the information you can about the current state of the market and your achievements for each of your profit centres. It will look at the competition and your relative position. Make sure that when you make a conclusion it is based on sound information, not speculation or hearsay.

Achievements

List achievements in terms of value, volume and trends. Look at distribution channels and sources of reservations broken down for each profit centre:

- rooms – and the different market segments
- meeting/function space
- restaurant/bar
- leisure.

Competition

- Which ones do you compete with? (Note: different hotels will compete with different segments of your hotel.)
- Their product and price comparisons.
- Is there any new competition?

SWOT analysis

- Strengths and weaknesses – against competition (try and be objective as you list bricks and mortar issues, but also image, staff and customer feedback).

- Opportunities and threats – market changes and external situations such as local economic development and exchange rates.

Where do we want to be?

This section is your opportunity to set some goals for the year ahead, both in terms of specific figures and more qualitative aspects such as awards. Think about your vision and how it can be fulfilled.

Sales targets

Set targets you want to reasonably achieve next year in each of your departments:

- rooms – by market segments
- meeting/function space
- restaurant/bar
- leisure.

It is notoriously difficult to make accurate forecasts of what might transpire next year. All you are really doing is stating some goals that you are going to make plans to achieve. If you forecast more room nights from corporate clients, this either needs to be based on interviews with the clients who confirm that their travel will increase, or based on your estimate that with a bit of effort you consider that you can sign up more clients. Ideally you would start from a zero base each year, since to just add arbitrary percentages to last year's figures does not imply that any real analysis has been made about the competition and the potential.

Qualitative targets

What you are trying to achieve next year:

- customer satisfaction comments
- awards for food

- ◆ guidebook entries
- ◆ star rating.

What do we want to change?

Before you start on your planning, you need to address the key strategic considerations. You need to stand back and decide whether or not what you are doing now is right for the future. It is useful to analyse your situation under product, price and promotion.

Product

Your evaluation of your own product and service and that of the competition will give you some ideas as to whether your offer is still appropriate for the current market or for any emerging market. Feedback from customers will provide much of the input for your consideration.

You need to look at bedroom and meeting facilities to check that you are up to date. If you have been losing restaurant covers despite your efforts, then maybe it is time to consider your whole offer, including the style and pricing. Are there any additional facilities that you ought to consider, such as fitness or leisure? Analyse your product under the three elements of service, environment and physical aspects as outlined in Chapter 1 pages 15–16.

Price

Sometimes it is possible to make a strategic leap rather than just looking at inflation. It could be that some prices could increase by 20 per cent if you can fill a particular gap by slight adjustment to your product. You might also be considering a new restaurant concept that needs an average spend 25 per cent less than your current level but will give you 50 per cent more covers.

If you keep your eyes open you will spot some encouraging signs within your operation. Maybe your wedding venue is booked at least a year and maybe 18 months in advance. If so, this is a major opportunity to look at your pricing policy.

Promotion

This is your opportunity to evaluate what has been working and what has not. Try and remove your personal preferences for particular tactics and look at your measurements. You need to keep a steady flow of new leads as well as making sure that you retain as many current customers as possible.

Taking into account the lifetime value, there is research to show that, in terms of return on investment, direct contact is the best tactic, followed closely by your own website, media relations, internet advertising and e-mail marketing. But this is only research and you will have your own statistics to help you.

◆ TIP ◆

Don't be afraid to make some bold decisions. If your sales specialist is producing results, consider hiring another. I know it's a significant cost but if they bring in at least ten times their salary, it must be a good thing. Especially if you cancel all those directory ads that you can't track.

How are we going to get there?

In this section you will look at any changes you need to make to your product and service and explore all the opportunities that there are for developing new business and maximising the revenue from current customers. You will consider your pricing and distribution strategy, select some tactics for new business and make some choices about resource allocation and budget. This is the place for the action plan.

Action plan

An action plan is a detailed list of all the action steps needed to carry out the strategies and tactics for reaching each goal. Below is an example of the sort of plan you need to make for each of the goals that you have decided on for the year. Ensure that your goals are all Specific, Measurable, Achievable, Realistic and Time bound (SMART).

Goal: To increase weekday occupancy from 60 per cent to 70 per cent within six months.

Strategy: 1 Develop 400 more room nights from residential meetings.

2 Develop eight more local corporate contracts to generate 600 room nights each year.

Tactics: Contact businesses to evaluate.

Contact booking agents.

Mail offer to venue finding agents.

Advertise in meeting magazine.

Update own website with special offers.

For each tactic you will need to decide who is responsible, what is the start date, what is the finish date and what is the cost.

Once you have planned the action steps to achieve all the goals for the year, you will also need to go through and make a month-by-month plan that incorporates all the various actions in date order.

Budget

Hotel owners are forever asking me how much they should spend on sales and marketing activity. My usual reply is to say that you need to spend as much as necessary to achieve your objectives. This may not be very helpful, but neither would it be much help to say that you must spend four per cent of your total revenue. If your occupancy was 40 per cent and you could increase that to 60 per cent by spending more money then I would recommend that you get on and spend the money. If at the end of the year you have spent, for instance, ten per cent of your total revenue on sales and marketing then you might take the view that this is a bit too much and look at ways to reduce it. But at least you now have the occupancy to work with.

If you take cost as the limiting factor, then you will be limiting your top line revenue potential. The key is in the evaluation and measurement and the amount you need to spend will depend on your own circumstances including your competition and location.

◆ TIP ◆

If you are one of a hundred hotels in a tourist destination then you will probably have to spend more than if you are the only hotel in a business park with a captive market.

As a matter of interest I think that on average US hotels spend around six per cent of total revenue, with hotels in Europe just behind at five per cent. Resort hotels tend to spend slightly more unless they distribute all their rooms through wholesalers. As with any averages there are some big deviations, particularly in franchise and chain hotels, that have to make a hefty percentage contribution for 'corporate' advertising.

One interesting development, particularly where you are launching a new hotel, is to use barter funds. This is where you use unsold room inventory as currency to stretch your marketing budget. This may well not be that new to you since it is likely that you already give away weekend rooms in return for radio advertising. There are a number of trading organisations operating in this field and you can use your credit to buy radio, TV and print advertising as well as printing services.

Measurement/evaluation

When you made your estimate of what you want to achieve for the year ahead, you will have used yardsticks such as market share, occupancy rates, average room rate by segment, advance bookings, customer satisfaction, repeat business, rooms per corporate client, advertising return, covers served, weddings booked plus others that you chose. You need to continually match your actual performance against what you expected, so that you can find out why you are behind or ahead.

If there are big deviations you may have to re-evaluate your strategy and take another look at customer feedback or the competitive situation.

◆ TIP ◆

A marketing plan must never be left on the shelf. It is a dynamic document that needs to be changed if the circumstances dictate.

Only change in response to the needs of your customers; never allow the plan to be curtailed by your accountant to improve the short-term bottom line. This is only likely to happen if the plan is not robust and well developed enough to deliver increased shareholder value.

What are the local opportunities?

Although this might seem an afterthought, the information that you gather here is vital. Your options for developing certain market segments depend on your knowledge of your local environment. For instance, you will not know if you can generate business from local boarding schools unless you have identified how many and where they are. The same is true for corporate business that relies on your identifying local business parks. Your yield management strategy will also be influenced by events that cause demand peaks in your area. You need to identify:

- ports/airports and stations
- shopping centres
- business parks
- major offices/employers
- universities/colleges
- schools
- hospitals
- defence establishments
- churches

- sports centres
- crematoriums
- registry offices
- government/council offices
- courts
- residential homes
- tourist offices
- local event calendar.

Cross check these with the customer types listed in Chapter 2 pages 44–63 and you will have a long list of potential to incorporate into your action plan.

Tools checklist

This list of 50 promotional ideas is useful to check that you have thought of all the ways that you could promote your business. I'm sure that you can think of more but they may provide the catalyst for some brainstorming with your team. To make any brainstorm session really effective have each participant think of at least 20 ideas (the first ten are easy and the next ten apply a bit of stretch to the imagination). When everyone has written their 20 ideas, go round the group one by one and ask for just one idea to write down on a flip chart. Keep going round the group until you run out of new ideas.

- advertising
- advertorials
- association memberships
- brochures
- bulletin boards
- calendar of events
- competitions
- co-op advertising
- coupons
- cross selling
- direct mail
- directories
- direct sales
- donations
- door to door
- endorsed mailings
- fairs
- fax back
- flyers
- follow-up letters/calls
- fund raisers
- gifts
- joint ventures
- local sponsorship
- loss leaders
- magazine articles
- newsletters
- newspaper columns
- newspaper inserts
- on-hold messages

- on-vehicle advertising
- piggyback mailings
- post cards
- press releases
- prize draws
- radio ads
- referrals
- signs
- special events
- sponsored events
- statement stuffers
- table cards
- taxi ads
- telemarketing
- testimonials
- trade shows
- t-shirt advertising
- web sites (other)
- web sites (own)
- 0800 number

KEY POINTS

- If you develop a written marketing plan you will probably be in the top ten per cent of all small businesses.

- Any action plan needs to be generated by you and your team working together. Involve everyone including kitchen staff and housekeeping.

- Set some realistic goals for your hotel, based on your competitive analysis.

- Your plan must be a live document, not produced and left on a shelf.

- Don't make the budget a straightjacket. Be flexible about expenditure during the year but evaluate every cost based on the likely return that should always be at least 10:1.

THE LAST WORD

If you have got this far then you should have a great marketing plan and be fully geared up to make a success of your hotel.

Unfortunately, even having this plan cannot guarantee your business success. There is a lot more to being really successful than just having a marketing plan.

In his seminal 1937 book *Think and Grow Rich* Napoleon Hill tried to sum up all those attributes that made the 200 American millionaires he interviewed successful. He tried to test out a 'secret' that Andrew Carnegie had told him was the foundation of his fortune. It would be impossible to try to summarise this book here. However there are a few interesting conclusions that I personally find fascinating.

The most important attribute of successful people seems to me to be that of persistence. For instance, Thomas Edison had to carry out over 10,000 experiments before he manufactured a successful incandescent light. More recently, Howard Scultz of Starbucks and Fred Smith of FedEx both had to endure years of financial problems before they were successful.

In order to sustain your *persistence* you need:

◆ **Desire**: A burning desire focused on your original idea can sustain you.

◆ **Plan**: A definite plan that highlights continuous action.

◆ **No negative influences**: A mind that is closed to all negative influences.

◆ **Help from coach or mentor**: Encouragement to follow through with your plans.

Other attributes that you need are:

- **Decisiveness:** Doing something is usually better than doing nothing. Mistakes are part of life and we need to make them in order to learn. Procrastination is bad not only for you but also for your team.

- **Concentration:** To make a success you need to concentrate on one thing at a time. Being a 'jack of all trades' will not help you beat the competition.

- **Understanding the power of the subconscious:** Your mind is very powerful but it needs to have constant positive input. Negative thinking can destroy ambition.

- **Cooperation:** You cannot achieve everything you want on your own. You need to surround yourself with positive people who can help you realise your vision.

More recently, some research has been carried out by the Cranfield School of Management and accountancy firm Kingston Smith. They polled owner-managers of 200 small to medium-sized business across the UK to try to find out the differences between fast-growing businesses and those in decline.

The attributes of the successful businesses were found to be:

- **Time in the business:** These successful owners actually worked less in the business.

- **Desire:** They still had their original passion for the business.

- **Concentration:** They kept focused on their core business.

- **Develop staff:** They invested more in staff training, had good financial incentive schemes and believed in the quality of their team members.

♦ **Business plan**: Owners worked to their original business plan.

♦ **New business**: Successful owners were always on the lookout for new business to replace natural attrition.

♦ **Competition**: They knew all about their competition.

♦ **The internet**: Successful owners used the potential of the internet to enhance their business.

♦ **Financial discipline**: They monitored their performance against budget, produced cash flow forecasts and maintained financial health.

So there you have it. A blueprint for a successful business! Nothing is ever that simple, but I hope that I have given you some things to think about. In all this you must keep track of your original vision, plan how you can run your hotel as a business and at the same time realise some of the rewards that you anticipated when you started out. Good luck!

Resources

This is not a comprehensive evaluation of all the options available for any of the subjects. These are resources that I have used, and you will need to make your own assessment as to their suitability for your purposes.

Autoresponder system for e-zines: Gary Ambrose
   www.emailaces.com
Keyword search: www.wordtracker.com
Benchmarking: www.bestpracticeforum.org
Business growth: Peter Thomson www.peterthomson.com
Colour advice: Angela Wright www.colour-affects.co.uk
Sales techniques: Jim Meisenheimer www.meisenheimer.com
Google ads: Perry Marshall www.perrymarshall.com/adwords
Telephone selling: Art Sobczak www.BusinessbyPhone.com
Direct sales: Dave Kahle www.davekahle.com
Body language: Albert Mehrabian www.kaaj.com/psych/
          Alan Pease www.alanpease.com
Hotel information newsletter: www.HotelMarketing.com
Open source software: www.opensource.org
Business process management (rate checking):

www.travelclick.net; www.ratetiger.com

Institute of Direct Marketing: www.thedma.org.uk

Cranfield School of Management: www.som.cranfield.ac.uk/som

Website link evaluation: www.alexa.com

Web link validator: www.weblinkchecker.com

Website problem solving tools: www.netmechanic.com

Web design software: www.nvu.com

Web browser compatibility check: www.anybrowser.com

Free information search tool: www.answers.com

Data Protection Act: www.informationcommissioner.gov.uk

The Institute of Direct Marketing. www.theidm.com

Chartered Institute of Marketing: www.cim.co.uk

Chartered Institute of Personnel and Development:
www.cipd.co.uk

Business lists: Experian www.experian.co.uk/nbd
Dunn & Bradstreet www.dnb.co.uk
AP Information Services www.apinfo.co.uk
Market Monitor www.market-monitor.co.uk

Online press release distribution: www.PRweb.com

Internet distribution outsourcing: Martin Philips –
www.recommendedhotels.net

Bartering: www.bartercard.co.uk

Open website directory: www.dmoz.org

Contact management software ACT!: www.sage.co.uk

Technology service provider: Pegasus Solutions –
www.pegs.com

Also check out the online sales and marketing resource that I edit at www.HotelSalesSuccess.co.uk. Here you will also find a link to my coaching and mentoring service at www.theHotelCoach.co.uk.

I would be grateful for any feedback or comments you have about anything in this book. Please e-mail me at editor@ HoteSalesSuccess.co.uk.

Further Reading

These books will provide you with more in-depth coverage of some of the subjects covered in this book.

Belbin, M (1999) *Team Roles at Work.* (Butterworth Heinemann)

Bird, D (2000) *Commonsense Direct Marketing.* Kogan Page

Blanchard, K and Stoner, J (2002) *Full Steam Ahead – unleash the power of vision in your company and your life.* (Berrett-Koehler)

Block, P (1990) *The Empowered Manager: Positive Political Skills at Work.* (Jossey-Bass Ltd)

Butscher, S (1998) *Clubs and Loyalty Programmes: A practical guide.* (Gower Publishing)

Cranwell-Ward, J, Bacon, A, and Mackie, R (2002) *Inspiring Leadership.* (Thomson)

Gilbert, A and Chakravorty, I (2002) *Go MAD about Coaching* (Go MAD Books)

Goldman, Heinz M (1958; 1993) *How to Win Customers.* (Pan Books)

Goleman, D (1996) *Emotional Intelligence: Why it can matter more than IQ.* (Bloomsbury)

Handy, C (1997) *The Hungry Spirit.* (Random House)

Hill, N and Alexander, J (1996) *Handbook of Customer Satisfaction and Loyalty Measurement.* (Gower Publishing)

Hill, N (1937; 2004) *Think and Grow Rich.* (Vermilion)

Hill, N, Brierley, J and MacDougall, R (2003) *How to Measure Customer Satisfaction.* (Gower Publishing)

Kotter, J (1990) *A Force for Change: How Leadership Differs from Management.* (Free Press)

Lewis, R and Chambers, R (1989) *Marketing Leadership in Hospitality.* (Van Nostrand Reinhold)

McDonald, M and Dunbar, I (2005) *Market Segmentation.* (Elsevier Butterworth Heinemann)

Mitchell Stewart, Aileen (1994) *Empowering People.* (Pitman)

Olins, W (1999) *Corporate Identity.* (Thames & Hudson)

Olins, W (2003) *On Brand.* (Thames & Hudson)

Owen, H (2000) *In Search of Leaders.* (John Wiley & Sons)

Pegg, M (1989) *Positive Leadership: How to Build a Winning Team.* (Lifeskills Publishing)

Peters, T (1985) *A Passion for Excellence.* (William Collins)

Schwab, V (1962) *How to Write a Good Advertisement.* (Wiltshire Book Co)

Schwartz, E. (2004) *Breakthrough Advertising.* (Boardroom)

Senge, P (1990) *The Fifth Discipline: The Art and Practice of the Learning Organisation.* (Doubleday)

Sugarman, J (1998) *Advertising Secrets of the Written Word.* (DelStar)

Wheeler, A (2003) *Designing Brand Identity.* (John Wiley & Sons)

Wright, A (1998) *The Beginner's Guide to Colour Psychology.* (Colour Affects Ltd)

Index

A-boards, 198
advertising
   internet, 180
   print, 170
airline crew, 45
associations, 46
average spend, 287

banners, 197
benchmarking, 31
body language, 140
Body Shop, 40
brand franchise, 65
brochures, 201

charities, 47
classification, 23

coach companies, 48
coaching, 104
coaching model, 104
colour, 6
commission, 239
commitment, 137
companies, 48
competition, 30
complaints, 140
consortium 65
copywriting
   adverstising, 175
   brochures, 203
   direct mail, 154
   website, 215
corporate identity, 4
customer priorities, 253

customer satisfaction
  measurement, 250
customer satisfaction surveys,
  255
customer share, 282

databases to keep, 257
delegation, 102
differentiation, 25
direct contact, 129
direct mail, 150
discounting, 248
distribution channels, 64

e-mail mailing, 160
emotional intelligence, 105
empowerment, 106

family, employment of, 97
features and benefits, 28
first impressions, 144

Global Distribution Systems
  (GDS), 70
good employee, profile of, 94
government, 53
groups, 53
guaranteed lowest rate, 242
guide books, 189

health services, 54
hotel booking companies, 73

incentive houses, 74
incentives, 114
incoming calls, 121
in-house promotion, 199
internet companies, 72
internet site, 206

leadership style, 76
leaflets, 196
lifetime value, 282
listening, 133
logo, 8
loyalty schemes, 260

marketing action plan, 290
marketing budget, 299
marketing plan format, 293
McCulloch, Ken, 41
media relations, 183
membership schemes, 262
military, 57

names, 5
negotiation, 134
networking, 147
news release, 187
newsletters, 165

organisational conflicts, 100
outgoing calls, 125

paper quality, 10

Pareto principle, 22
photography, 205
positioning, 26
posters, 198
pricing policy, 231
pricing psychology, 232
psychographics, 24

rate checking, 241
rate parity, 241
rate segments, 236
rate tactics, 240
referrals, 273
registration forms, 258
representative firm, 68
request for proposals (RFPs),
    240
reservation network, 67
restaurant offer, 20
retention, 288
revenue development, 284
room product, 17

sales activities, 81
sales person attributes, 92
sales promotion, 194
sales specialist, employing a,
    87
sales resistance, 135
schools, 57
segmentation, 23

senior citizens, 5
show business, 58
signage, 12
special events, 278
sport, 59
symbols, 9
systems, 268

taglines, 10
team commitment, 94
team success, 99
testimonials, 276
time management, 83
Tourist Boards, 59
typography, 8

unique selling proposition, 27
universities, 60
up-selling, 280

venue finding agencies, 73
Virgin, 39
vision, 37

weddings, 61
weekend visitors, 55
wholesalers, 74
wording, 10
work/life balance, 85

yield management, 243